Home and Belonging
Collected Life Stories of Foreign Women Married to Nigerian Men

Edited by
Kanchana Ugbabe & Joanne Umolu

Tharros Books— Jos, Plateau State, Nigeria
ISBN: 979-8-218-08502-5
Library of Congress Control Number: 2022918812
Title: Home and Belonging: Collected Life Stories of Foreign Women Married to Nigerian Men
Editors: Kanchana Ugbabe & Joanne Umolu
Digital distribution | 2022
Paperback | 2022

Cover Design by Ijimbli Odaudu

Appreciation

We wish to thank all the women who contributed to this book. We appreciate them for their time and effort to write down their experiences in order to share them here.

We are especially grateful to our Nigerian husbands. Without them there would have been no reason for this book.

Table of Content

Introduction
Kanchana Ugbabe & Joanne Umolu

One is drawn to Edwidge Danticat's claim that 'all immigrants are artists because they create a life, a future from nothing but a dream.' (Joe Fassler. *The Atlantic*, August 27, 2013) They are confronted with the 'blank canvas' of a foreign country. Brushstroke by brushstroke, they build a life bringing the artistic enterprise to fruition. It is an intervention fraught with risks but rich in imagination. This is the life of the exile, the nomad, the immigrant.

This book brings together life stories of women who are immigrants with a difference. They come from diverse parts of the world, they are married to Nigerian men, and choose to make Nigeria their home. Most of the women have lived in Nigeria for about 40 years, some longer.

Cross cultural marriages were an anomaly in the early days, particularly in the 1960s and 70s. There was so little information about Africa and a lot of misinformation. The colour and race issue too stood in the way of women from Europe, North America, Russia and Asia establishing long-lasting relationships with African men. There was resistance and estrangement from family and community on the one side and a sense of uncertainty as to what lay on the other side. Some women left what was 'home' and crossed the oceans with their husbands to make a dwelling in Nigeria. Others met their husbands on neutral ground, in a third country. The journey to Nigeria in this case was a return 'home' for their husbands but was the start of yet another adventure for the women concerned. In most cases, the marriage, and life thereafter involved a journey into the unknown.

The writing shows the vast differences, geographical and cultural that the women have had to cross and traverse to settle in Nigeria, raise families and be productive in terms of employment. Some women were fortunate to have guideposts, manuals in the form of husbands and relatives who led them by the hand and introduced them to the intricacies of culture. Others stumbled their way through the woods, learning from mistakes, humbled and bruised but holding on.

Women in the UK faced racism and racist attacks in the 1950s when they first met and married their Nigerian husbands. Astrid and Elizabeth write of the racism they encountered in the UK and of the courage and determination that made them hold on. 'If I am to live in the desert, I will follow him,' was Astrid's decisive statement in 1962.

Veronica's (Scotland) speaks of her experience of polygamy as a cultural artefact and then closer to home, as a personal experience. As wife no. 1, she had to come to terms with the idea and reality of a second wife who would share husband, home, and resources. It is a nightmare scenario for the foreign wife but one which finds tacit acceptance in the community. 'She will get used to it,' was the verdict. Kenna (Canada) sees her life in segments intersected by 'silver threads', the people who added meaning and value to her experience of Africa.

Kathleen (UK) overcomes all odds to live in a remote part of Nigeria, Gwoza in the North East, with her husband, a pastor, who along with the community spoke only Hausa. Kathleen soon became conversant in the language. She walked long distances or travelled on the back of a bicycle to most places in the hilly terrain. Kathleen's story includes the ride on the back of a motorbike to the hospital, on a rough road, to give birth to her first baby.

There are civil war experiences which Pat (UK) and Joanne (USA) write about. Joanne also documents the anxieties experienced during the pogroms of 1966 when Igbos in the North were hounded and killed. Fleeing the home with her Igbo husband and children and seeking refuge in a school compound is an unforgettable night of terror. Pat experienced the horrors of the civil war first hand. War experience came with dislocation, deprivation, and the anxieties of protecting and providing for children. Families are separated during the war, there is fear and uncertainty, the foreign women manage the homefront and face the future with scraps of courage left.

Road travel on the 'night bus' becomes a metaphor for the journey of life, the discoveries, the insights. Sarah Chuwang (USA) documents her life as a politician's wife, a life intersected by military coups in Nigeria, her husband's detention, and separation from the family for a period of time. Jane (Canada) immerses herself in her Nursing career as well as the Yoruba culture of her husband while raising a family in the university city of Ile-Ife.

Lack of privacy, and living in close proximity with the extended family in Nigeria is a challenge to most of the women. Eliane's (France) adjustment to sights and sounds and tastes so foreign to the French town from which she hails is woven into her story of Nigeria. Natalia's (Russia) encounter with snakes in Nigeria as opposed to dolphins (her passion) makes an engaging story. Kanchana's (India) writing oscillates between what is lost and what is gained in merging with the second culture. Jewellery played a big part in her Indian culture but seemed negligible in her Nigerian setting. She talks of transitioning from a caste-defined Indian society to one in which everyone was happily treated as equal. Agness (India) finds herself in the Igbo village (before her husband joins her), surrounded by the extended family and community whose intentions she is unsure of. Her story records her fear of the unknown, the moments of terror.

The women write of the generosity of Nigerians, of being welcomed into family and community. As they grow and mature in Nigeria, they appreciate the kindness of people, and establish a bond with the community. The community in turn appreciates the 'distances' the women have travelled and recognizes the services of some of the Nigerwives. A few among us have even been given chieftancy titles in appreciation of the contribution made to the community. Katia (Italy) starts a school in her husband's village. Through donations from friends in Italy she is able to award scholarships to the students and enable them get a good education.

The collection bears witness to the enterprising spirit of the Nigerwives. Joanne grew up in a quiet, farming community in Midwestern USA but she successfully coped with what life offered her during frequent political crises in Nigeria, became an educationist, and currently runs a school for children with special needs. Astrid gained experience as a travel agent and managed her private travel business in Lagos and Jos. Kenna started off as a nurse and midwife and grew in commitment and experience to become the Country Director of the Canadian Development Agency (CIDA) in Abuja, Nigeria. Other women among us have blossomed into artists, writers, interior decorators, entrepreneurs, and professionals in their chosen field.

The stories form a rich tapestry of women's lives. They come from the heart and convey a whole range of feelings and emotions. They are stories of growth and awareness. The migration from Europe,

Asia, and the United States to Nigeria is a continuous flow. Women continue to travel and migrate on account of love and commitment. The hurdles and impediments are many, the reward is an enriched life among strangers who become family. Kinships are forged in unlikely places. Roots are put down and lives nurtured. Wherever the women come from, home and belonging are ultimately in one place – Nigeria.

Liminal Spaces

Kanchana Ugbabe

I imagine myself a star in an Indian movie, one of those tear-jerking Bollywood creations, so dramatic, where fiction becomes fact, and there's love and romance followed by tension…and a pot of gold at the end of the rainbow. I was in the habit, even as a child, of stepping aside and watching me say my lines and choreograph my movements. When later, my cinematic life unfolded in Nigeria in all its technicolour, I saw myself as a seasoned actress playing multiple roles. The world around me was framed shot by shot. The camera angles were poised and focused as my visual narrative evolved and the drama took shape.

My personal narrative moves from Madras, South India, where I was born and raised, to a life-changing transition in Adelaide, Australia, where I met my Nigerian husband, to Jos, Nigeria where I matured, and my horizons expanded. It is a time of growing and maturing, searching, and finding meaning. I look back to my time as a graduate student in Adelaide, Australia in the early 1970's, a Resident Tutor with a larger apartment instead of a conventional dorm room. It was here that I brewed my coffee in a percolator and agonized over my cultural adjustment as a twenty-three-year-old, fresh from South India. The feminist movement and the counter-culture movement gathered momentum around me and engulfed me in their tide. The *sari* clung to me in cold and warm weather. I groped and floundered but a certain youthful confidence sustained me.

When you have crossed the oceans and moved from one continent to another, Asia to Africa, via Australia, what is it that pervades the writing? There is intense nostalgia, perhaps, as we tap into memory recalling sounds and smells. Many write in terms of loss, loss of privacy, loss of possessions, loss of a way of life, loss and distancing from things and people dear to their hearts. Displacement and dislocation. But what of the extraordinary accretions, the extra dimension that unfolds to one's view of the world?

In the liminal space where I find myself, I have a unique angle of vision from which I explore life in a way that an expatriate or visitor to Nigeria would not be privy to. It is also a space in which the Nigerians (the owners of the culture), too familiar with their physical and social environment would not find themselves. It is a liberating space, a space of keen insights. I insinuate myself into its crevices; I embrace the culture creatively. I write my journey and my search into my own stories.

An image that also comes to mind is of a tight rope walker in a Russian circus. As a child my parents took me to the visiting Russian circus in a huge circular tent. I held my breath watching the tightrope walkers and the pole-walking act. Walking a tightrope has its risks but it also has its thrills. It is a balancing act where you have to be so poised, so still, yet trembling between the abyss and a thin place. There is skill, an instinctive negotiation with the unknown, an anxiety bordering on excitement.

Jos, Nigeria, is on a high elevation, nestling in the Jos plateau, surrounded by hills. I throw the blankets aside and crawl out from under the mosquito net and rub my palms together for warmth. The cooing birdsong rouses me from sleep together with the crowing of the rooster in the compound. The air is chilly and crisp. I grope in the dark and find my way to the kitchen unbolting numerous doors and turn on the solar lamp before putting the kettle on to boil over the gas stove. Electricity is scarce and water is stored in a bucket. Other early morning noises filter in – the chatter of women as they take their metal buckets down to the tap, gates opening and creaking shut. Dogs barking as security guards who have been on night shift retire to their homes at daybreak.

In Madras, South India, the ceiling fan swirls overhead. I sit up on my low bed. From my bedroom window, I can see the coconut palms towering above, the banana and jack fruit trees in my father's compound. I hear the milkman at 5:30 dropping the milk packets in the receptacle on the veranda. We share a fence with Madam Janaki, the owner of the food business, who's rasping voice jolts me awake in the early hours of the day as she shouts at the servants to wash, clean, and start the cooking. The whistling of the milk boiler is followed by the hissing of the pressure cooker. As the morning unravels, Madam Janaki's instructions get more difficult to follow, the servants begin to drop the stainless-steel dishes, her voice rises a pitch, the blenders, grinders, and pressure cookers respond with great urgency. The food smells good over the fence but Madam Janaki is hard to please. The servants are always late; the coconut chutney needs a touch of tamarind paste, and the carrot *halwa* is short on spice. Is it oil or water you think you are pouring into the saucepan, she screams. Do you know the price of oil these days? The cook gets told off that he is fit for the street-side café not her restaurant as he had mixed a bit of flour to thicken the curry. Madam Janaki switches from Tamil to Hindi to even the occasional instruction in English, "Okay, okay, da. You shut up and get out fast!" I am wide awake by the time Madam Janaki in her hoarse voice rolls off the menu to the cooks and servants, "How about *sambar* with *drumstick* and *brinjal*? Can you manage that? Then *rasam, pappadams*, cabbage *poriyal* and cauliflower fry…"

Jos is a lovely city in central Nigeria. It is reported that Queen Elizabeth on an early visit to this area in the 1950's said, "This is a little piece of England in Africa." People habitually build on rocks in this city which is dotted with large and spectacular granite rock formations. It is not uncommon to see huge boulders sitting amidst trees and shrubs in the yard. Occasionally, a boulder is left in the middle of a courtyard or dining room, and the walls chiselled into shape around it. It was a tin-mining town in the old days. The abandoned mines seasonally fill up with rain water and have come to be called 'mining ponds'. Being 4,000 feet above sea level, with a temperate climate, it became a favourite spot for colonialists and missionaries to establish schools, hospitals, churches, and even a local jailhouse built of stone. The old homes have fireplaces for wood fires. Jos is the capital of Plateau state which has about 40 ethno-linguistic groups.

Jos was most welcoming of me as my husband and I settled down in our little home, in the mid-1970s, grew vegetables in the backyard, kept chickens, and had two dogs in the compound. It was also in this innocent little country town (and in Zaria, a few years prior to this) that we started a family and I began my career as a university teacher. Everything was new and fresh to me but also charmingly quaint and inviting. When we were graduate students in Australia, my husband showed me a postcard of the market in Jos. I responded, "It is beautiful!" seeing the colours of the vegetables and the clothes people wore. "Beautiful? It is a market!" he said, sharply. I was seeing the market as a spectacle, I realized. Seeing it through the lens of a tourist and an educated Asian. I learnt years later that beauty and functionality went together in Nigerian culture. That art is produced not to be gazed at but to be 'used' – the pottery dish I bought in the market, the intricately woven mat, the decorations on the outside of the mud huts in my husband's village in Benue State. Everything had its purpose and its place and was not 'beautiful' for its own sake.

It seemed strange at first but I became 'Our Wife' to the relatives and friends who came to visit, a term that bestowed on me a sense of belonging in my husband's Idoma culture, a claim as a 'communal wife'. I learned to shop in the market in Jos, buy meat and fish from the open stalls, and fruit from the Hausa fruit seller, and in the process, develop a camaraderie with the people I met every week. They called me *bature* and sometimes, the variant *oyinbo*, which were the terms used for 'foreigner' in Nigeria. I gleefully responded to their elaborate Hausa greetings:

Ina kwana? How was your night? (How did you sleep?)
Lafiya lau   Very well
Ina gajiya? How is the tiredness (fatigue)?
Ba gajiya   There is no tiredness (fatigue).
Yaya iyali?   How is your family?
   (The implication being spouse and children)
Lafiya lau   Very well
Yaya maigida? How is your husband?
   ('the owner of the house' or the head of the household)
Lafiya lau   Very well
Yaya yara? How are the children?
Lafiya lau   Very well

In my short story, 'The Silver Toe Rings' (T*he Flinders Jubilee Anthology*, Adelaide, 1991), the narrator interprets the greetings as being ambiguous: 'She felt accepted when the Hausa vegetable seller greeted her elaborately, enquiring in stages and in order of priority the welfare of her husband, her children and her household. She felt pleased when he addressed her as '*uwargida*', the wife of the home, but slightly disconcerted as the word also stood for 'first wife', implying perhaps that others may follow' (p.303).

Much as it told me that the culture revolved around family, I also began to understand the hierarchies within the family. My position as 'Our Wife' came with responsibilities towards the extended family, and expectations that I would bear children to perpetuate the family name (boys in particular), but also to increase the clan numbers. I became anxious about having children. An elderly relative's comment on first seeing me was: "She is skinny with small hips. Are you sure she can bear children?" Cross-cultural marriages could be a hit or a miss as I discovered later. Fortunately, the family I married into was warmly receptive of me and accommodated my curious ways of seeing the world.

I missed my mother when I got pregnant. She would have fussed over me as they do in India, treating the pregnancy as a 'delicate condition' with specially cooked foods and keeping me happy with pretty gifts and pleasant sights. I didn't have the traditional Indian bangle ceremony when the bangle man would arrive with his boxes of coloured and gold-speckled glass bangles, there would be fun and food and laughter and every woman invited to the ceremony would have a set of glass bangles of her choice on her wrist to take home. I, as the mother to be, would have my wrists laden with bangles of all colours…

Karen King Aribisala in her book *Our Wife and Other Stories (1990)* writes fictionally and symbolically about a Nigerwife (a foreign woman married to a Nigerian man) participating in a family funeral. The foreign wife wore a lace wrapper as was expected for the occasion; as she danced the sharp edges of the lace cut into her heels which began to bleed. She kept dancing and shedding blood, grieving for her loss of home, her element. 'It (the lace) cut its edge into my alien unaccustomed flesh, until every movement was agony', says the foreign wife in Aribisala's story. In my own short story 'Exile' (from my short story collection, *Soulmates*) I write about the protagonist embracing, and being embraced, but it is out of sync with what is going on around her. The embrace into the culture as an 'insider' is also simultaneously a rejection of the 'outsider' for breaking a code of conduct. In another of my stories, 'Blessing in Disguise', a foreign wife ('Our Wife') ruminates over her future home with a co-wife in a polygamous arrangement, and their triangular relationship as a threesome 'in front of the fireplace'.

During the early years of marriage, in Nigeria, I wanted to deny myself everything external, everything that was me, just to be accepted. I gave up my *saris* and started wearing Nigerian *wrappers*. The headgear was always tricky, I could never get it right, so I gave up on it and left my hair uncovered. The odd fusion-status probably drew attention but I was oblivious to it. I learned to cook with unfamiliar ingredients, hot pepper, melon seeds, the bitter leaf, palm oil, black-eyed beans, and others. From having grown up a vegetarian, I ventured into cooking all kinds of meat, goat, grass-cutter, chicken, and fish. 'Bush meat' dried in the sun was a speciality in my husband's Idoma culture of the Benue people. Special visitors to the home were honoured by having bush-meat-pepper-soup served to them. Where did the courage come from? Pounding hot, cooked, yam in a wooden mortar until it became pliant and elastic, and soft as butter was an artistic enterprise. I sought the assistance of young nieces until my husband bought me a Japanese contraption designed for the purpose! This 'yam-pounder' churned the yam into mashed-potato-consistency and took a fraction of the time and effort. My superficial cultural negotiations kept me happy and content. It was like donning a decorative mask that gave me freedom to observe from behind the papier mache, without being seen. I was 'trying', the relatives commended me, in good humoured fashion. Mishaps and blunders were tolerated without stern disapproval. Some men took their foreign wives by the hand and led them as tour guides into the intricacies of culture. I stumbled my way in the woods receiving hard knocks and learning to grow a thick skin. As with women around the world in survival situations, writing came to my rescue.

Formality pervaded all interaction in the Nigerian society I became part of. People made speeches, stood up and addressed a family gathering, gave formal advice, received visitors with an established set of greetings and exchange of pleasantries. Women, young and old stood up to speak at assemblies. Families regularly had 'meetings'.

Men and women had titles by which they were addressed before being spoken to. (One of my husband's titles is 'Elephant-killer', even though he has never approached an elephant, I am sure). In the Idoma culture, funerals were preceded by an 'inquest' into the death of the individual - a theatrical performance where formal questions were posed and elaborate responses given as to how and wherefore the death had occurred. Traditional weddings were like unrehearsed, spontaneous stage performances, the stating of the bride price by the groom's family, the entreaties on the part of the bride's family, and the happy outcome. Women's voices rang out loud and clear and women were heeded to, when they spoke. In polygamous households (of which there were many in the extended family), the first wife spoke on behalf of her co-wives, she gave instructions, distributed the provisions, and organized the daily routine. It was a hierarchical society where age was respected. I observed it about me with awe and admiration. The women among the relatives spoke with wisdom and authority, took decisions, and kept their families together whatever the circumstances. 'Every married woman is sitting on a six-inch nail,' my mother-in-law once said, 'It is when she raises her bottom that you discover the damage.' Sitting tight-lipped hoping for divine intervention to bring relief was a suggestion, yet.

Is 'home' a place of origin, or is it a destination, a place of refuge, perhaps, or a condition of the mind? Are the affiliations different for men and women? Growing up in South India, home was where my parents lived. I could not imagine that space without them. It would not bear that name. But in Nigeria, 'home' referred to ancestral origins, to where your clan came from in the patriarchal line. It was not a house that you built or lived in but an area, a region. People travelled 'home' for Christmas, traditional weddings and funerals took place at 'home' rather than in the city where you lived. My notion of home, on the other hand, evolved as I travelled the world, the configurations changed. A sense of belonging, a set of objects that constituted putting down roots - these were the redeemers in the journey. I had had a 'home' of sorts in Adelaide for five years – I could still recall its architectural features and the view from the kitchen window. The presence of husband and children was central to my definition of 'home' for the rest of my life's journey in Jos, Nigeria. My family anchored me and gave me my foundations. I had an official home address in Edinburgh, Boston and New York City where I have lived with my family at various times.

Every time I visited my parents' home in Madras, after my emigration to Africa, there were awkward pauses, silences concerning where I was coming from. No one asked me questions about where I lived in Nigeria, the people I lived amongst, the food I ate, or the way my day was configured. I could tell from their chattiness that they imagined the worst, whatever that was. Theirs was such a closed, caste-endorsed, Hindu unit. I, who had been nurtured in their midst, had broken all codes and stepped out to God knows where. 'Love marriage' (as opposed to arranged marriage) was taboo in the Indian society of the 1970s. There were no bridges to connect my Indian family to my way of thinking. There was no common denominator from which our conversations could flow. It took a while to ease myself into their routine, a hot, cooked breakfast, shopping for *saris* and jewellery, a three-course lunch, siesta, evening coffee and *tiffin*, visits to the temple, and late dinner before crashing in bed. I had forgotten that adults drank warm milk like babies before going to bed. The TV serials kept everyone anaesthetized for most parts of the evening. Ganesh (the resident *chef*) cooked up a storm and the wonderful outcome, aromatic curries, *chapatis* and chutneys appeared on the dining table at regular intervals. I enjoyed with relish my old way of life unfurling before me. I took on the lead role. A part of me hidden away somewhere surfaced with each visit. Tamil, my birth-language, tripped off my tongue with ease.

The bedroom I retreated to was strangely not my space anymore. This was where I had sat by the window and pored over my physics and chemistry texts before the exams. Amma would breeze in at unsuspected moments to check if I was really at my books or staring out of the window at neighbourhood boys on the terrace of the home next door. The built-in cupboard that had housed my school uniforms, and later my *saris* looked quaint and dusty with silver fish darting back and forth. Old black and white photographs lined the walls. There was the scent of incense and moth balls in the air. The Godrej bureau, the creaky metal apparatus had stood in its spot all these years. This was the vault, the safe-deposit which housed the gold and diamonds, and delicate silver ornaments. The door to the bedroom was shut before the Godrej bureau was opened, lest the servants catch a glimpse of the contents and get ideas in their heads! Amma would sit on the bed and bring out the velvet-lined boxes one by one. In hushed reverence, she would give me the jewellery to try on. There were so many bits and pieces, screws and clasps, pearl ear drops, and my favourite, the diamond earrings shaped like a pair of fish. This was my mother's world and from time to time she gave me privileged access to its interior before she locked it all up and tucked the key bunch on her hips. My short story, 'The Silver Toe-Rings' gives a glimpse of this world.

A free-standing cupboard with netting for sides was lodged in Amma's dining room. The four legs of the cupboard stood each on a concrete moat which had water poured in regularly and fortified, to prevent ants from crossing over! The cupboard was called the 'meat-safe' (in a vegetarian home), something the colonialists had devised for storing sweetmeats. I cherished this cupboard as a link with my childhood. It too was kept locked when the servants were around.

My South Indian society was deeply entrenched in an age-old class system that drew sharp divisions between 'them' (the servants) and 'us' (those who hired them). In my Nigerian home, on the other hand, the boundaries were not so boldly drawn. People engaged in domestic help merely played a role; they were not subservient, nor were they treated as second class citizens.

Material possessions in general, and gold jewellery in particular, mattered little to me in my adopted Nigerian culture. I tossed them on the dressing table or carelessly put them together with knick-knacks bought in the market. This attitude, (learned and acquired over the years), was based on the fact that in African cultures everything seemed negotiable. Possessions belonged to everyone and to no one in particular. If you held on tightly to something, whether it was clothes or money, it might outlive you! One had to assume a casual attitude towards possessions, learn to release them if the need arose. This went hand in hand with a sense of responsibility towards others. A person's responsibility was not only towards his or her immediate family but also towards brothers, sisters, cousins and the amorphous extended family. The bank account it seemed, was useful, but more so when it served the needs of the family at large and the community. It was people and relationships that mattered. You derived significance from the people who thought well of you for your generosity, looked up to you for guidance, and depended on you. These were lessons I learned gradually.

On one of my visits to Madras, I took out my books, Camus, Gunter

Grass, and Dostoevsky and arranged them on the rosewood desk in my parents' home. There was an instant feeling of 'home' once the books took their place. I lived out of the suitcase for a week trying to ease myself into the South Indian culture that had a faraway taste in my mouth, and the feel of invisible restrictions that hedged me in. Amma tucked the jasmine strands in my hair. I had outgrown the little veranda where I sat screened by the metal awnings. Curtains parted and the lady in the house across the road peeped. The families that had lived alongside us, the people whose children I had played with and had gone to school with had all sold their homes and moved elsewhere. Property developers had built apartments in place of quaint little independent houses. The trees of my childhood had grown enormously spreading their branches overhead, providing shade for the entire street. They bore witness to a time gone by, a time of little beginnings and a humbler way of life.

I burrow into the tunnels of my mind; I weave my way through the alleyways of memory like the protagonist's search for Zaabalawi in Naguib Mahfouz' short story of that name. It is a maze where certain 'spots of time' stand out. Memory and the passage of years have blunted the rough edges of some experiences while others take on a visible radiance. I see my life in frames, as black and white photographic shots.

When I was a child we spent our holidays in Thatha's house in Rajapalayam. It was a small, rural town in South India, surrounded by paddy fields and mango and coconut groves most of which were owned by Thatha, my grandfather. His was the grand old house in the town, stretching for quite a length of the street. An archway at the top of the street announced the entrance to Pannayar House. The house was always full of family members, visiting, getting married, having babies – everything seemed to happen there. There were dependents, servants, cooks, and maids in attendance, and a bullock cart with two bulls hitched and ready for the visit to the market or the temple. Thatha rode horses, entertained European visitors, owned a double-barrelled gun, and had his own apartment within the compound. Achi, my grandmother was a gentle soul, a small woman who sat in the Second Room and read the National Geographic magazine and The Illustrated London News which Thatha subscribed to besides others. Her father had been a minister in the colonial government. She was home schooled and was an avid reader. She wrote postcards to family members in English in ornamental flourishes and curlicues. She knew very little about cooking or housekeeping having lost her mother as a child, but the house ran itself and everyone seemed to know his or her place. The sound of Thatha's wooden clogs on the cold floor twice a day as he walked through the grand house to the dining room at the far end put everyone on edge. Women scuttled like mice behind pillars and doors. He stopped to talk if the rustling of the *sari* distracted him or the bells in the toe-rings tinkled. It was usually one of the daughters hesitantly asking for money, or for the use of the bullock cart for an outing somewhere.

Color had never negatively impacted our cross-cultural marriage or my day to day life as an Asian in West Africa. If there were differences in our cultural outlook, color did not enter into it. It was just a statement of fact. Blackness was the norm, and there was no need to affirm it, defend it, or flaunt it. But the India I had grown up in was color-conscious. As far back as I can remember, face powder 'lightened' our faces and Amma would send us to the mirror to 'put powder' on our oily faces. There was 'Fair and Lovely' face cream for women who could be transformed from 'dark' to 'fair' in seven days. The monolithic view of beauty was reinforced by the TV advertisement which showed the mutation of the woman emerging 'fair' and glowing after using the product. The prospective bride in the matrimonial advertisement had to be 'fair' and slim. West Africans on the other hand advertised a locally made black soap to rejuvenate the skin and rubbed camwood to give the skin a sheen and a glow. (In more recent times, some Nigerian women have taken to bleaching their skin with face creams, and straightening their hair). The bride in Calabar, Nigeria, was sent to the 'Fattening Room' a month or two before the marriage ceremony to be properly fed, shaped, and equipped for the occasion.

The colonial presence in Africa had generated labels by which the 'white' man or woman' was referred to in the local languages. The Akan in Ghana gave the name *oburoni* to those who had come from distant lands. The foreigner was called *mzungu* in the Bantu language in Eastern and southern Africa. *Toubab* was the term the Gambians and Senegalese used for the rich traveller who also happened to be a foreigner. In Nigeria, it was *oyinbo*, the 'white man' or 'white woman'. It was purely descriptive and did not carry any derogatory connotations. As a brown South Asian I still came to be called *oyinbo* by the neighbourhood children. I acquired the status of 'Ma' or 'Mummy' through my long association with the culture but the 'white woman' label, ironically, was difficult to shake off. Bi-racial children are called 'half-castes' in local parlance, (like the Japanese '*hafu*'), though our son claims he is actually 'double-caste' in terms of richness of experience.

Bi-racial children are the life-rafts in cascading waters. They are blithely secure and free of the thorny issues surrounding cultural adjustment. They fit comfortably into the world they have grown up in and enjoy the benefits of their dual cultural inheritance. Our children have a stronger sense of belonging and community and relate easily to the members of the extended family. They are more innovative and resourceful and are not constrained by the lack of amenities or the apparent confusion. The millennial, bi-racial children are the *metropolitans*, citizens of the world!

I saunter through the mnemonic chambers, the vestibule, the central nave, the transept locating rhythms that draw me back to a place called home…

On one of my visits to Madras, Appa and I take a walk to the grocery store at the entrance to the housing estate where my parents lived. Cows lie supine in the middle of the road chewing rose garlands and banana leaves fished out of the street bin. Milking time is over. The women sit at the junction with baskets of jasmines, stringing them on strips taken from the banana stem. The fragrance of jasmine mingles with the flavours of cardamom-filled carrot *halwa* in the *mittai* shop nearby. The place comes alive in the evening as people pull up in motor bikes, cars, and auto-rickshaws to buy the hot savouries and freshly fried syrupy sweets. We walk back slowly avoiding potholes, garbage dumps and reckless drivers.

Madras is a city of relics and fond memories now – a city where I once had friends and a life. A city choked by air pollution, where the familiar landmarks are fast disappearing as buildings get torn down and streets get dug up for the metro rail. Young people crowd into fast food outlets, vicariously experiencing life in Europe and America. Modern conveniences have taken the place of the vegetarian eatery at the street corner and the local coffee shop. It is my city, Madras then, Chennai now, but I have to navigate my way through it as a traveller in a strangely familiar landscape. Politicians and movie stars (sometimes rolled into one) have become the gods of the new millennium. The long and the short of it is that I have grown older, the environment has changed and I together with it. I am not the naïve college girl of yester years.

Naming children after people you love and respect is a custom in Nigeria. It is hoped that the children named after you, will take after you in character and conduct. You, the adult, had an unspoken responsibility towards the children named after you. When a young graduate student invited me to his wedding, I discovered to my surprise that his Nigerian bride bore my name. How did a Nigerian woman come to have an Indian name? Heart-shapes in glitter encircled the names of the bride and groom on invitations, banners, and postcards. At the wedding, we met the bride's father who apparently had also been my student twenty-five years previously. The young man had taken my literature courses at the university, and on graduation and subsequent marriage, had named his baby daughter after me! This young girl at the age of twenty-two was marrying another student of mine! Stranger than fiction! Since then, there have been several children named after me growing up in different parts of the country. It seemed that my cultural merger was complete!

I recall the monsoon rains falling in sheets in the Madras of my childhood. Rain without wind. It is as if a million taps had been turned on, the water just pours like silk, like oil. The air is thick and heavy and steamy. People and cars, auto-rickshaws and motorbikes negotiate the flooded roads, the potholes, and the flooded drains to get to work. The mynah bird coos towards late evening when the rain has subsided. It gets high pitched and insistent as the evening wears on.

Home is where your security lies, where you are enveloped in belonging as daughter, wife, mother, writer. It is where tightly knit kinships are strengthened and new relationships formed and forged. It is where the oceans of the mind meet and borders and boundaries collapse instinctively.

My experiences overlap from post-colonial Madras morphing to Adelaide, Australia, to Jos, Nigeria and home and belonging become fluid spaces of the mind.

There are no Dolphins in Nigeria

Natalia A. Anigbogu

I was born in the Soviet Union, USSR, the country that no longer exists. When I was four our family moved from a small town in the southern part of the country to a fast-growing industrial town further north which is within Russian Federation presently. And it was there, while finishing school, I decided I wanted to study dolphins. In the early 1970s the research on dolphin studies were widely popularised with claims of their high intelligence, their friendliness towards humans and their ability to communicate. I envisaged my future by the seaside wearing those cute knee trousers, checkered shirt, and carrying portable ultrasound devices for translating dolphin speech to human speech (Russian of course); or on a boat playing with dolphins who were eagerly entertaining me by leaping out of the water and gliding on the sea waves.

My ambition to study Dolphins was interrupted, however, when I met and married a Nigerian medical student. We moved to Nigeria and settled in Jos, the capital of Plateau State. The city of Jos is four thousand feet above sea level. It features multiple, beautiful rock formations, has exceptionally pleasant weather, and a whole lot of snakes. And so, here comes my encounter with snakes during my early married life and beyond when Nigeria became my home.

During the first five years I did not see any snakes except inside the local zoo and wildlife park, but those were huge and kept in specially built pits. The first snake I saw was a green one. The children and I saw it in our living room, green, with beady black, innocent eyes; it tried to hide from us. The screaming, jumping up on the couch and running helter skelter alerted my husband who was just about to leave for the hospital for work. He was visibly annoyed by such unexpected drama on our part. He sent for someone nearby who promptly killed the snake with a machete. That was a signal to the snake community in the area to try their luck in and around our premises. Subsequently,

Hanatu, my domestic helper, claimed that she often smelled snakes and had to deal with those who entered the garage. Once I encountered one when there was no one else in the house and I was afraid it would crawl somewhere where it would be difficult to find if I went for help. Even my mother who was visiting from Russia was confronted by snakes when she was alone with my baby daughter. Another time, as my husband entered the bathroom, he saw a shifting grey mass inside the toilet tank which dove into the toilet bowl. Although we later poured poison in the toilet, for a long time we were always fearful whenever we were near the toilet.

Eventually we bought a beautiful piece of land and built our own house on it. The land was close to an extended stretch of rock formations and even though the place looked beautiful, I expressed my concerns about the snakes. But my husband assured me that the people living around that area told him there were hardly any snakes there. However, soon after we moved into our house we had a frightening experience. Around eight o'clock in the evening, my husband came back from the hospital and our son went out to open the gate for him. Unfortunately the security lights outside went off briefly and in that short period of darkness a snake bit him. My husband managed to kill the snake and then rushed into the house to get a razor blade. He quickly used the blade to make an incision on our son's foot and allowed the foot to bleed before we rushed him to the hospital. We took the dead snake with us in a glass jar. The doctor on duty did not identify the snake and he did not administer an antivenom. The leg got swollen twice its normal size. The doctor administered some medication and to our great relief after a few hours the swelling started to go down and we went home.

In the years that followed we had a lot of unwelcome visits from the inhabitants of the rocks, not only snakes but also scorpions, one of which .stung Hannatu. One evening as I was on the way to turn on the generator, I saw a green snake with beady black eyes under the rose plant. Both of us jumped in different directions. I told it to go and bravely proceeded to the generator house. On the way back the snake was no longer there.

Mostly the snakes were outside the house, but a few found their way inside. But what forced us to try to block all entrances to our house was an encounter with a cobra. My husband and I had been preparing to attend a function around Christmas time. I was putting the finishing touches to my outfit. My husband was ready and about to go out to the car when he heard a shuffling sound behind the shoe shelf. He called our son to push the shelf out from the wall and find out what was behind it. And it was our son once more who had to face a snake. This time it was a small cobra (small by cobra standards) which spat in his eyes. I came out to see that my husband had cut the cobra cut in pieces and our son was washing his eyes under the tap. An urgent call to an ophthalmologist whose instructions we followed saved the day and our son's eyes. The outing naturally had to be cancelled.

My husband is from Idemili Local Government of Anambra State in South Eastern Nigeria. The people of Idemili regard the python, *Eke Idemili*, as a representative of their deity and therefore, a custodian of their culture and tradition. A visit of the snake to people's homes could mean different things as the snake is said to have the power to bring good or bad tidings. It is a non-poisonous python, and it is treated with utmost respect and dignity. It is forbidden to kill it.

Recently our son posted some pictures on Facebook that he took during his visit to a snake farm in Nasarawa State in Nigeria. It was a python on his shoulder and wound around his neck. Maybe he is trying to close the gestalt.

I am still afraid of snakes though and I am yet to close my own gestalt connected to dolphins. I recently bought a brooch and a couple of earrings in the form of dolphins. May be that is the closest I will get to dolphins.

At Home
In War and Peace

Patricia Otonahu Kanu

I have just celebrated my 80th birthday, surviving my younger sister, who died at age 70, and my mother, who passed away at the ripe old age of 93, less than a year later. Further family tragedies and life experiences have also taken their toll on me. I lost the youngest two of five children, my daughter, at the tender age of 20 and my son at the age of 48. My darling husband died after 54 years of marriage. I lived through a civil war in which we lost my mother-in-law. For much of my life I have faced the challenges of having to grapple with a variety of cultural differences as I moved around the globe.

I was born on 7th April 1941 in Leicester, England. My mother was a domestic servant. Our father disappeared during WWII so she was left to bring us up on her own, finding work where she could as not everyone would take on a woman with two young children. Before I was nine years old, we had lived in four different houses in which she'd been a parlour maid and then housekeeper. She taught us to ride a bicycle, manage on few resources and make the best of what life presented us with – excellent lessons for my future as it turned out!

My sister and I were very excited when we finally moved into a house of our own in a small Northamptonshire village - one room downstairs, one bedroom and an outside kitchen with no running water and just a tap in the yard shared by us and two other households. The toilet, fortunately with water, was at the top of the garden.

At the high school, I developed a love of languages when I started learning French and then Italian, with Latin thrown in for good measure. If I smelled a continental cigarette, I would walk behind the person smoking it, hoping to hear a foreign language. I'm sure this interest in other languages/cultures helped me settle more comfortably in the many foreign countries I later found myself.

I gained admission to Birmingham University where my life took an unexpected and, as it turned out, amazing turn. I had only been on the university campus for a few days when I passed a student in the corridor of the Faculty of Arts building where we were both studying. Our eyes met and we nodded to each other. The next time I saw him we were lunching in the same cafe and he came over and said hello. I learnt he was reading English Language and Literature, his name was Okoro Kanu and that he was from Nigeria. At the time I had no idea where on earth Nigeria was. Little did I know then that not only would Nigeria be my home for more than 30 years, but my new Nigerian acquaintance, Okoro, would become my husband. As it turned out we fell for each and despite our very different backgrounds we got married.

At first my mother had not been in support of our marriage. I had led a comparatively sheltered life up to then when suddenly I wanted to marry the first black person my mother had ever met. Apart from being black, he was from a different country and twelve years older than me. Thankfully, my mother eventually gave her blessing.

Although Okoro and I were happily married, racist attitudes prevalent in society made life difficult for us. Once, before we were married, I was asked quite openly, "How's that wog friend of yours?" This was the time (1960's) when "No blacks, no dogs, no Irish" and "Blacks go home" signs appeared all over London where we lived. Mixed marriages were considered abhorrent by many in England. A man in my village had likened it to a cat marrying a dog.

Racism created financial hardships for us which we felt most acutely as the babies started coming. Catering for our growing family however was especially challenging because the employment opportunities for Okoro were very limited. Even with his Honours degree and previous experience as a qualified teacher, he was considered too well qualified to be put on the non-professional register, but was told he couldn't go on the professional one because he was black! It was therefore up to me to get a job while Okoro looked after our two children. The only one I could find quickly was with the Intercontinental Telephone Exchange where at least I could use my French, as all calls were either in French or English. Fortunately, he got a teaching post before long which paid more money and I became the homemaker again.

Our life changed dramatically towards the end of 1964 when Okoro was offered an appointment by the Federal Government of Nigeria. For him this meant an end to his struggles in London and a joyful return to his home country. The children and I were to follow once he had found suitable accommodation for us all. As we hugged goodbye and his train left for Liverpool from where his ship would depart, I was filled with a mixture of grief and trepidation, not knowing when I would see him again and apprehensive about the big changes that were soon to take place in my life.

Okoro had tried to prepare me for life in Nigeria while we were still in England. He had given me the Igbo name, Otonahu, with the expectation that his family members would come to know me by that name – and they did! He had even begun to teach me to speak some Igbo, yet nothing had prepared me for the culture shock I experienced when I landed at Lagos airport in December 1965 with two toddlers and a 7 month old baby in tow. I had barely had a glimpse of my husband when a host of his relations suddenly appeared and swarmed around us in an exuberant welcome. We felt quite overwhelmed by it and the journey from the airport to our new home remains a complete blur to me, save for the joy of knowing that we were once again reunited as a family. Unfortunately, my hopeful expectation of a private moment with my husband after almost a year apart had to remain on hold when I discovered my home was filled with still more people waiting to see us. We were greeted with traditional dancing and clapping as Okoro proudly introduced us to his large family and close friends.

To help me settle into my new life in Lagos, Okoro thoughtfully arranged for a relative to come to the house often in case I needed help. I appreciated having her around as she amused the children and explained to me the different foodstuffs and the customs.

We had been living in Lagos for about four months when my mother-in-law arrived – presumably to inspect her new daughter-in-law. She spoke as little English as I did Igbo and refused to take anything from me unless I handed it to her with my right hand, in accordance with Igbo custom. She really annoyed me one night when I had just fallen into a deep sleep to find her shaking me awake and beckoning me to the front room to go and close the window – obviously considered by her the wife's job even though she and my husband were still up and chatting together. My husband, noting my "annoyance", told me to go back to bed. He must have explained our rule, that the last one to bed closed the windows, because she never disturbed me again. Honestly it was quite a relief when Okoro took her back to her village, several hundred miles east of Lagos!

A military coup had taken place in January 1966 but it didn't really affect my life as I was getting used to so many different things – climate, country, food, customs and the various local intonations when speaking English! Another coup in July brought a new military ruler to power and rumours started circulating about killings in the north of the country. As the rumours became more widespread, our relations started leaving for our hometown, Arochukwu, in the East of the country. We were expecting our fourth child and although there were stories of many atrocities being committed, we thought they were exaggerated and weren't unduly worried until we saw an Igbo lady living nearby being dragged away by a group of soldiers – she never returned!

By the time our son arrived on 23rd December 1966, the situation had deteriorated to such an extent that we no longer felt safe in Lagos so Okoro asked for a transfer to the Eastern Region Ministry of Education. Consequently, come the end of February 1967, we were on the move again, this time to Owerri, a small town in the Eastern Region. As dawn broke, our little family unit left Lagos for the next chapter of our lives, hundreds of miles away. Okoro was to begin lecturing at the Advanced Teacher Training College in Owerri where luckily, we had been allocated the last vacant bungalow on the college campus.

We continued hearing personal accounts of atrocities committed against easterners, particularly in the North, and on 30th May 1967 the Eastern Region seceded from the rest of Nigeria and the new Republic of Biafra was born to widespread rejoicing. In June 1967, we moved to a bigger house which I hardly had time to enjoy before we were hit with the dramatic announcement, on 7th July 1967, of the declaration of war on Biafra by Nigeria.

The English Principal of the College informed me that British wives were being repatriated and asked if I wanted to join them. I said I needed to discuss with my husband before I could make a decision. Okoro said it was up to me and he would go along with whatever I decided. I could leave with the children, leave without them or stay as we were. Clever man – on my own head be it! I returned and told the Principal that I would sink or swim with Biafra.

The fact that there was a war on didn't make much difference to our lives in Owerri until one Sunday in August when we heard a plane flying overhead. Next minute we heard explosions .and still didn't realize what it was. Our campus was some distance from the town centre where the bombs had landed, otherwise many of us might have been killed. Okoro counted 56 bodies in the mortuary and also noted that the majority of the people were caught by shrapnel from the knee upwards. From then onwards, he gave us frequent drills on taking cover in a prone position, protecting our heads with our arms.

One day the children rushed to tell me that there was a white man at the door in a long white dress. There weren't many white people around apart from a handful of us women married to Biafrans and certainly no white men. I therefore wondered who it could be, especially a man wearing a dress! It turned out to be a very wonderful Catholic priest who was, at that time, in charge of the Holy Ghost Missionaries in Biafra. These missionaries were Irish Catholic priests and sisters scattered throughout Biafra with its high concentration of Catholics. We weren't Catholics but he was calling to check that we were all well. I have been told that out of the 2000 plus expatriate wives at the start of the war, there were less than 20 when it ended, many of whom received help from the Irish missionaries, regardless of their religious beliefs.

While we were in Owerri, I would write a few lines to my mother any time I heard of anyone travelling out of Biafra. I never got a reply so had no way of knowing if she had received them or not. In fact, she went for about 15 months without receiving a single word from us, with only pictures of starving Biafran children in the newspapers to bring her "comfort" and making her wonder if her own grandchildren were in the same appalling condition.

This was why the Reverend Father's contact with us was all the more precious because it was through him and the Irish Reverend Sisters that we were able to make contact with my mother again. I don't know which was more wonderful – me hearing from her or knowing that she had got a letter from me and therefore knew that we were still alive and kicking!

My mother kept all the letters she ever received from me during the war. It was fascinating, years later, to see the many postmarks on the envelopes – Gabon, Equatorial Guinea, Ireland, Switzerland etc. as well as many different places in England.

As time went on prices soared and it became increasingly difficult to manage. I used locally made washing soap for the clothes and dishes. Flour became so expensive we had to go without bread. I just coped the best I could and it was only after hearing planes overhead and/or bombs exploding that I was truly frightened for our safety and wished we were anywhere else but there. That feeling would soon pass as one or other of the children needed my attention – and life would continue!

September 1968 arrived. I heard some deep booming sounds but wasn't too worried, thinking it was shelling from our own side. On the 15th, an army officer told us it was enemy shelling and advised us to get out of Owerri as quickly as possible. This posed a big problem because our car wasn't roadworthy due to lack of spare parts and we had no other means of transport. Okoro told me to pack some essentials while he went to see if he could make arrangements for a vehicle to take us away from the town. He came back with another lecturer who would transport us in his small Volkswagen Beetle to a safer place. There was already a passenger in the front with the lecturer and the boot was filled with their belongings. It was immediately obvious that the "essentials" I had packed were far too many. We squeezed in the back – my four children and me, my handbag, a plastic bucket and a small bag with some flour, powdered milk, dried egg powder and a bit of sugar. I remember thinking that at least I had some milk for the children to drink and I could make them pancakes for breakfast the next morning. But did I have anything for them to drink out of, a frying pan or any oil for the pancakes? Maybe those were in the plastic bucket but I couldn't remember because everything happened so quickly. As we were about to drive off, Okoro pushed two raffia mats through the window and across our laps saying "You better take these darling. You don't know where you'll be sleeping tonight!" I hadn't really given that a thought but I didn't have much time to think of everything when I was asked to pack the essentials accumulated over the previous 2-3 years into a bucket and a small bag with air raids thrown in for good measure!

We eventually turned off the main road and travelled along a sandy, bumpy track for a couple of miles before being deposited at a small, completely bare school classroom. If I say it was 12 feet x 12 feet, that might have been generous. It had a cracked, concrete floor and of course, electricity and running water were non-existent. If I thought I had had problems before, they were nothing compared to what I now faced. My first thought was for water. Where was the nearest supply? I discovered that it was a good mile away and I only had one bucket! If I used that to fetch water, half of it would have spilled by the time I got home because I couldn't balance it on my head like the local people around. What was worse, if I used the bucket for storing water, I would have nothing to bath the children in, nowhere to wash dishes (did I remember to pack any?) and nowhere to wash the clothes (but we only had what we stood up in!). How could I even go to the stream and back with the children then aged 7, 5, 3 and 21 months? It was certainly too far for the younger ones and they were all too young to be left unattended and in a strange place. Even if, by some miracle, I did get to the stream and back, there was the problem of boiling the water for drinking since streams could be used for bathing, washing clothes and as toilet facilities for humans and animals in the absence of any other source of water in the area. To boil water I needed a fire which meant firewood and matches – and did I have any container to boil water in – kettle, saucepan or even a tin? Maybe I had a frying pan with which I had hoped to make the pancakes – but how much water would that hold? Exhausted, I rolled out the raffia mats on the concrete floor (no pillows!) and slept for as long as possible, hoping that things would look different in the daylight.

Learning to light a fire was one of the most frustrating problems I had to face in the 'bush'. There were no newspapers, kindling, or the firelighters I was used to in England – only a lot of smoke to choke on once the fire caught. Times without number I got a face full of ashes and/or smoke as I blew to get the fire going. If the fire didn't get a good hold before I started cooking, the food tasted smoky. If the cooking pot didn't have a lid or I forgot to put it on before blowing the fire, the food in the pot got covered in ash, and when it was all I had to feed the family we ate or starved. Matches were scarce so I had to keep puffing to make sure the fire caught properly. Controlling a wood fire involved more than turning a knob to raise or lower electricity or gas. If the food boiled too quickly, the bottom of the saucepan burnt which of course affected the taste – and there were no scouring pads, only tufts of coconut and/or sand to get it clean. Actually, in the absence of anything else, these were very effective.

Fortunately, Okoro reached us safely two days later with a suitcase, one or two pots and pans and some foodstuffs. The suitcase was a real godsend because it served as our table and was the one and only "piece of furniture" that we had.

My poor European back really suffered! I was used to doing jobs in an upright position – at the sink, the cooker, the table – and sitting in an armchair and sleeping in a bed with a mattress. After a week or so of bending over for every little chore, I told my husband, "I'll never take a bed for granted again!" I would go to bed with a backache and wake up with it. There were no pillows either so one had to sleep on one's arm – and I always woke up several times during the night with pins and needles.

Toilets were another problem. The children and I had to get used to a latrine, literally a deep hole in the ground that one stood or squatted over. I was absolutely petrified that one of the children would fall in so I had to accompany them each and every time. Many hours were taken up each day going back and forth with them.

By early October 1968, less than a month after arriving in the 'bush', we went up in the world and acquired two single bed frames, 6ft x 2ft 6inches. Of course, there were still no mattresses. We pushed them together and put the raffia mats across the springs to provide a bed for me and the children. Okoro slept on another mat on the floor.

Obtaining money posed quite a problem. The nearest bank was about ten miles away and with no car, Okoro either had to walk there and back or later cycle when we somehow acquired a bicycle. He would leave well before daybreak since the banks only stayed open for a couple of hours. Even after going all that way, he often reached the bank to find that no money was being given out or at best, just £2 or £3 per customer, regardless of the balance in one's account.

By this time, we had moved into an almost completed house belonging to the local headmaster. We had been allocated two rooms – wonderful except for the empty spaces all round our limited furniture. But it really was wonderful to have a separate room for sleeping. We hadn't enjoyed our spacious quarters long when the army requisitioned the headmaster's house and we were forced to move again, this time to two smaller rooms in another local man's single-storey dwelling. This meant new sleeping arrangements. I and the four children aged 9, 7, 4 and 3 still lay on the raffia mats on the two single bed frames pushed together, but by then two nieces were with us. They slept on mats underneath us as the room was too small for them to sleep on either side. Our so-called "front" room was partially divided by a raffia screen. The smaller portion was where we kept our kitchen "equipment" – pots, pans and foodstuffs, while Okoro slept on his mat in the main part of the room. The place where we did our cooking was behind the house and shared with our host's family.

Life was increasingly hard as 1970 arrived and with it the announcement that Biafra had surrendered. While hugely relieved, we still faced many problems as our Biafran money dwindled and we had no way of getting any more. By the end of January, one of Okoro's younger brothers and a cousin, both ex-Biafran soldiers, had come to join us. I was grateful for their presence as women were being grabbed by the victorious soldiers and taken off to who knew where. I wondered if Okoro would be asked to return to work in Lagos. Would the children at last start school? The two oldest had not yet spent a day in school due to the war but we were confident that our maths and writing lessons with them in the sand would hold them in good stead. Happily, they appeared to have suffered no ill effects from their hitherto strange education and eventually started school in the classes they would have been in anyway.

We returned to Owerri and were allocated a 3-bedroom bungalow but with no electricity or running water. Cooking was still done outside with firewood. We had a lovely kitchen with built-in cupboards and Formica worktops. Even though the unit drawers were missing, it was still heaven after managing in two tiny rooms for 18 months. In April 1970 electricity was restored and the children couldn't understand how it could be on in different rooms at the same time. It seemed magical to them and their excitement lifted my own spirits too.

I started working with the Red Cross on a voluntary basis and then with the Christian Council of Nigeria (CCN). In September Okoro moved to Lagos with his brother, having been reabsorbed into the Federal Ministry of Education. Finding accommodation there took time and December arrived with us hoping that we could spend Christmas together. Somehow, he made it back to us – bringing a letter and parcel from England, the latter containing presents for everyone as well as photographs of my mother, my sister and her family. I gazed longingly at one particular photograph of a snowman in my mother's garden as perspiration dripped from me!

Okoro returned to Lagos after Christmas and we finally joined him about three weeks later, to see the beautiful 3-bedroom flat he had found for us. We enrolled the children in school and on 1st February 1971, I started work at the CCN in Lagos until the arrival of our fifth child, on 28th December 1971 to complete our family.

In November 1972, I got a job as a ground hostess with UTA French Airlines where I could once more practice my French language skills. A perk of the job allowed me to bring my mother to visit us in Nigeria at a nominal cost. Words cannot express how wonderful the five months she spent with us were, after so many years of not being able to see each other. Suffice to say Nigeria was a real eye opener for her but the best part was to see the joy on her face as she played with her grandchildren. After my mother returned to England and life began to feel a bit more secure, I joined another French company with whom I stayed for a total of 13 years.

In 1975, my husband was sent on study leave to Stanford University, California. Before he left, I asked him to teach me to drive so that I could be independent and not have to rely on others to drive me everywhere, particularly in a medical emergency. Okoro's stay in America was for one year initially and we both felt it would be better for me to remain in Nigeria where we not only had accommodation, but I had a good job and the children were settled in school. When his stay was extended to three years however, I decided to join him and even though our first daughter stayed behind to complete her secondary schooling, she later joined the rest of the family and we were all grateful for the opportunity to experience American life. This was another culture to acclimatize to – anything and everything available in the shops, no haggling over prices, everyone cycling safely on the university campus and even going further afield once we got a car. I did manage to get my own American driving licence after mastering the different rules and road signs, and also took some business classes at a local college.

We returned to Nigeria in August 1978 and my husband was posted to Jos, hundreds of miles north of Lagos but with a much more agreeable climate for me. Sadly, I was not able to enjoy this for long because two incomes were required to support the family and, unable to find suitable work in Jos, I had to return to my previous employer in Lagos. The children also had adjustments to make with a different school system – and different rules! No longer the more casual attitude that they had grown used to in California with pupils calling their teachers by their first names, no school uniform, a wide range of subject choices each term and no harsh disciplinary measures for lateness or answering questions incorrectly etc.

We saw each other as often as finances permitted until Okoro was eventually transferred back to Lagos and normal married life continued once again. My next job was with the EU at their delegation in Lagos, first as a liaison officer and later in administration. While at the EU, I was able to travel to the Commission HQ in Brussels and meet others from Delegations around the world, thus bringing together my love of all things foreign.

Okoro retired from the civil service, joined a private company and continued work on his book "The Pre-British Aro of Arochukwu" (eventually published in 2000) which he had started during his sojourn in America. Come 1997, his knees had become very bad due to arthritis and he travelled to the UK for operations on both of them. He was about to return to Lagos when he collapsed and was admitted to hospital, where heart problems were diagnosed. I had thought I would be spending the rest of my days in Nigeria but "Man proposes, God disposes" so in 1998 I returned to UK to join my husband.

Although I was born and bred in the UK, I had lived a very different life for the previous thirty-three years and it took time for me to get used to this land of plenty and literally years before I stopped worrying about washing dishes/clothes while the water was still running - or ironing before the electricity was cut off! The big advantage was that Okoro and I were together and since our daughters were all now settled in the UK, we enjoyed getting to know new grandchildren and taking pride in their achievements. Although Okoro would have loved to return home, he accepted that his health required reliable and constant medical care which meant staying in England where we remained in happily married bliss until his death in 2015.

Although my three children and eight grandchildren are now scattered around the world, we remain very close. Recently we came together to celebrate the marriage of my oldest granddaughter. So the family continues to grow. I'm in regular contact with them all as well as with my many Nigerian in-laws, thanks to modern technology. While I now wonder how I managed all those years without modern conveniences, I've had a joyfully fascinating life and am thankful for all those who helped make it so

On the Road

Sarah Chuwang

I have travelled in my car with my driver to many towns in Nigeria. When travelling on Nigerian roads one must pass through frequent police checkpoints. Typically, the policemen operating such checkpoints demand car documents, frustrate drivers with questions and delays and eventually allowing them to pass through. However, once on our way to Abuja when were stopped at a road block after showing our car papers as requested, the policeman asked me for documents showing that import duties had been paid on the car I was riding in. Needless to say, I had no such documents with me and thus began a standoff. After an argument and questions back and forth about what I was going to do about the situation, the officer told me that he had no choice but to take me to Kaduna where I would be charged to court for not having the customs documents. I told the officer to go ahead and do as he had threatened. The police officer climbed into the passenger seat of the car and off we drove towards Kaduna. I started reading from some spiral bound folders next to me. Eventually the officer asked why I was not disturbed about appearing in court. He was also curious about the contents of the documents I was reading. I told him I had been commissioned by the Government to write a report on human rights violations on the highway. He immediately told the driver to pull over and stop the car. He wanted to know why I had not told him who I was, and accused me of wanting to get him fired. He rushed out of the car and I continued on my journey to Abuja.

On another occasion, we were stopped at a checkpoint and told to pull over. I remained in the car, while my daughter and the driver got out and tried to determine why we were being detained. After about fifteen minutes, I took a wrapper and a pillow, got out of the car and laid down underneath a nearby tree. The officer asked my daughter what I was doing. She feigned ignorance. He came over to ask if I was sick. I told him I was not, but that I had left early in order to get to Jos before dark. I told him I was tired and if anything happened to me on the road because he had delayed me, my blood would be on his hands. After hearing this, he told me to get up and go and "take my trouble" with me!

I have only travelled by bus to Lagos once. On the way, the bus driver stopped in a remote area for a regularly scheduled break to allow passengers to relieve themselves. I am of the generation in which modesty was emphasized so I went quite a distance away from the road and eyesight of the driver. I had finished and gone back to the road only to discover the bus in the distance ascending the hill. A few villagers who were on the road began to point at me and the hill where the bus had now disappeared from my view. Somehow, I was not too worried, as I knew someone would eventually raise the alarm when they had noticed I was missing. Sure enough, the bus returned and picked me up, and I became the brunt of many jokes for the rest of the trip. That was the first and last time I successfully relieved myself in the bush!

Goodbye Italia…Hello Nigeria

Katia Bartolomei Ekesi, *Ugoma Abatete*

I was born in Italy in 1942 and grew up in Rome. There were four of us in our family; my father, who was a lawyer, my mother, myself and my younger sister, Rosita. During the summer vacations my sister and I used to travel to Viggiano to visit our grandmother. In my grandmother's house was a huge library and we would spend hours there going through the books. We were particularly fascinated by the medical books belonging to my grandfather who had been a medical practitioner. This inspired me to plan to study medicine after completing my secondary school studies. I wanted to enroll in the Medical Faculty at Rome University, but there was no provision for me to live on the campus and the Medical Faculty was a bit far from where we lived. I had been longing for a car of my own and thought this would be a good excuse to ask my father for one. But to my great disappointment my dad told me that I could not have a car until I graduated from the Medical School. I then considered the option of studying law as the Law Faculty was nearer and I wouldn't need to attend every day. I was faced with a dilemma of whether to become a lawyer like my father or follow the footsteps of my grandfather and become a doctor. I finally decided to read law.

Indirectly my father helped me to make my final decision. It turned out to be a good choice as I was able to take up a job during my studies and from my first salary I bought a Fiat 500 on a hire purchase arrangement. I was happy.

I had my car, my job and I was a University Student and … I was in love!!!! I graduated in April 1970 as a Doctor in law.

I had met Dominic Ekesi in 1963 in Rome at the University where he was studying Civil Engineering. We fell in love and we began to consider a future together. Since we were planning for marriage, I wanted to introduce Dominic to my father. Not an easy task!! An opportunity to present an African to my father as a prospective marriage partner arose when, in the course of his work, my father met the Ethiopian leader of a delegation for a joint project with Ethiopia. Fortunately for me my father liked and respected this African gentleman. I took advantage of this situation to arrange to introduce Dominic to him. We were hopeful when he agreed to meet Dominic. But to our great disappointment he refused to approve our marriage. Sadly, this was the first and the last time they met!!!!!

However we went ahead with our marriage plans. Dominic had decided that at the end of his studies he would go back to Nigeria which would mean I would have to be prepared to leave Italy and live with him in Nigeria. He suggested that it would be good for me to travel with him to visit Nigeria before we make a final decision to marry. This would give me the opportunity to know the country where I would be going to live for the rest of my life. I eagerly agreed and we prepared to travel in August 1966.

My journey to Nigeria turned out to be very interesting. I had experiences which were beyond what I had imagined. We were booked to fly on 27 August 1966 when Alitalia informed us that all flights to Nigeria were suspended because of a state of insecurity resulting from a military coup. Out of my total ignorance, without any consideration of risks involved, (I was young and in love) I just wanted by all means to travel to Nigeria despite an unstable political situation in the country. My leave had already been approved by my working place so, come rain or come shine, I was determined to travel within the period that I already planned for. Alitalia resumed flights four days later and Dominic and I flew together to Lagos on the first available plane.

My arrival in Nigeria at the Lagos airport is still very vivid in my memory. Immense heat welcomed us at the airport on our arrival. The air was hot and humid. One single ceiling fan swirled above the immigration officers on duty. This was the only source of ventilation. The interior of the airport vibrated with heat, everywhere was total disorder. All the passengers rushed at the same time to the bench of the immigration officer. It was chaos and mayhem. *Quite an experience!!*

Getting out of the airport, we checked into a hotel. We had planned to stay for a few days of sightseeing in Lagos before proceeding to Dominic's hometown, Abatete, in what was then the Eastern Region. Our hotel was a middle class kind of hotel. We were not able to afford a luxury hotel, naturally. We were checked in to a room on the ground floor. We felt safe as there were burglary proofs on the windows. Below the windows was a desk where we kept our valuables. (No experience!) Dominic's wallet must have attracted some unwanted attention on the other side of the windows, as on our third day his wallet suddenly disappeared from the table.

This experience contributed to a dampening of my spirits as we began our "fact finding journey" of Nigeria. Subconsciously it affected me. The sight of abandoned children on the street playing near dirty smelly open gutters, the unrelenting presence of mosquitoes in the evenings and the theft in the hotel were far from the warm welcoming experience I had expected.

However, I tried to take it all in good faith. I was looking forward to meeting my future husband's family. After all, love conquers all. With this new mood of expectancy, we were ready to leave for the hometown of my future husband. Dominic had been away from his hometown for more than six years. We knew that on his arrival he will need to pay full attention to his mother. Therefore he asked a cousin to accompany us and to stay with me whenever he had to leave me to take care of his home duties. At last we were on our way to Abatete. When we finally left the main road, we took a taxi to the village. To reach the house we had to drive through a forest of very tall palm trees. It wasn't easy to drive the six kilometers on an untarred road during the rainy season. Suddenly a very tall man appeared stark naked with a chain on his arm and leg, He crossed the road and disappeared again, completely naked. Dominic explained that he was a mad man. That was the height of my African experiences so far. Suddenly I realized that I was alone in Africa without my family and that I would live a totally different life and adapt to a totally different culture. This would be necessary for my survival on this strange continent. Would I be able to cope with it?

In such a frame of mind we finally arrived at the family house. The taxi driver off loaded our luggage and left us. At that moment I realized that my only means of getting back to the city had gone!! Everybody was excited to see their son Dominic returning from abroad with a white girl, but I could not say a word. I just started to cry: I was sobbing uncontrollably despite all efforts by the family members to calm me down. I was in shock and it took me some time to calm down. Gratefully the family understood my situation. They had sympathy for me and tried to comfort me. Despite all this "intermezzo" I decided to stand by my future husband. I stayed in the village for about a week. I had to get used to people coming just to look at me, the first white woman they had ever seen. Little did I know at the time that years later I would not be a curiosity, but rather a women fully accepted in the community and honoured with a chieftaincy title.

We returned to Italy and after an engagement lasting four years we got married on August 12th 1967 at San Marco Catholic Church in Piazza Venezia, Rome. We moved to Milan where Dominic got a job with an international Company.

We returned to Nigeria in September 1972 and by that time we already had two children, Cristiana Akubunachi and Roberto Chidobe. (Our third child, Maximiliano Emeka, was born in Lagos in 1976.) The first few weeks after our arrival were particularly challenging for me. Dominic had started work with Agip, an Italian oil company, and could only take us in the car for shopping on the weekends. In the meantime, I had to find food for the family. For about a week after our arrival in Lagos, we had to depend on street sellers who passed near us to supply us with food to eat. We bought plantain, bread and fruit and this was sufficient for the time being. I was trying to get into the rhythm of Lagos local life

Considering my poor knowledge of the English language, my prospects of finding a good job were poor. Therefore I knew I had to be innovative. In those days there were large communities of Italians, French, Greeks and Lebanese in Lagos. I got a bright idea of how to have my cake and eat it too. I would become a distributor of Italian magazines. This way I could keep in touch with my homeland by reading the Italian news and, of course, make money. My dream was to open a bookshop with books and magazines imported from Italy as well as from France and Greece. My major challenge was that I was required to personally collect the magazines which meant I had to travel.to the airport to meet the planes at inconvenient times.

While I was engaged in this activity an Italian expatriate gave me the idea of importing luxury furniture from Italy which he was sure there would be a market for in Nigeria. This prompted us to establish a company, Better Living Ltd, through which we engaged in furniture production and distribution. Before long the company became renowned for the construction, importation and promotion in West Africa of high quality furniture of Italian design. The activity in the furniture industrial sector fulfilled our dream. I enjoyed promoting the importation of Italian products in Nigeria and my husband, on the other hand, was proud to manage the factory in the outskirts of Lagos where he could provide training and work for hundreds of his countrymen.

However, I was soon finding it difficult to cope with running the family business and raising our three children at the same time. It was quite demanding. Therefore I decided to invite my mother, Mrs. Silvagni, to come to live in Nigeria for an extended period to help take care of the children. My mother retired from her government work in 1982 and joined us in Nigeria where she lived from 1982 until 1994 when our last child entered university.

Our children had been attending school in Lagos. But with the arrival of my mother we were able to enrol them in Hillcrest school in Jos. We rented accommodation for her and our children in Jos and she adjusted beautifully to Jos life despite her limited English. For several years, before we hired a driver for her, she drove herself, coping bravely with the Jos traffic. Jos residents admired this Italian grandmother when they saw her in the market bargaining with her limited English. She was a brave, hardworking lady… my backbone!! She helped us to develop our business indirectly. We are ever grateful to her for her selfless sacrifice to bring up the children to make them successful God fearing human beings. She left us finally in Rome on the 14th December 2011. Even if physically she is no more with us, her impact was enormous. She is and will be always in our heart!!!! I considered myself a very lucky person as not every Nigerwife had such a privilege.

In 1980 my husband came along with me to the Immigration Office in Lagos to processes my Nigerian Passport. The Officer openly showed his surprise at seeing both of us together. He commented that normally it is only the expatriate wife who presents herself to apply for the Nigerian passport as a result of a broken relationship with the Nigerian husband. I got my Nigerian Passport in 1982 signed by President Shehu Shagari.

Since our life in Lagos was organised thanks to the help of my mother, I was able to focus on community development projects in my husband's village. As a result of my involvement in Abatete, I earned their appreciation and admiration. According to them it would have been a blessing if every foreign wife should be like "Katia Ekesi". It made me feel very good and further stimulated me to do more for the community. "Win-win".

I was actively involved in the rural electrification project at Abatete from 1975 - 1980. At Christmas in 1979 I was in Abatete with my husband to lay the foundation stone for Abanna Girls Secondary School. This gave me the idea of inviting the Reverend Sisters of Saint Caterina of Sienna, a Dominican order based in Rome, to establish the first convent and co-educational secondary school in Abatete. In addition, through a joint effort by my friends we were able to give out about 40 partial scholarship every year to the more brilliant but unprivileged students from Abatete.

In a recognition of my efforts the Igwe of Abatete HRM, late Chief Patrick Plume Eze Edeogu 1st, gave me the title *Ugoma Abatete* on the 29th December, 1994. This was the first time in Abatete that women were given a Chieftaincy title. Four of us received a title that day, myself and three other ladies from Abatete. My title means a beautiful Eagle of Abatete who brings good things to the village.

Ageing naturally slows someone down, but luckily I am still a very active person surrounded by my four grandsons in Lagos and enjoying my two granddaughters in Austin, Texas where my youngest son lives. I am active in all these charity and professional organisations: Nigerian American Chamber of Commerce, Lagos Chamber of Commerce and Industry-Nigeria British Chamber of Commerce,- Rotary Club of Victoria Island, International Women Society, Lagos, Lagos Motor Boats Club, Ikoyi Club, life member of IBB Golf Club, Abuja. And of course, I am a senior member of the Lagos Nigerwives Organisation. It is always good to travel back home to Rome, Italy.

But the real home is where your family and close friends are. Therefore naturally I have a very strong sense of belonging to Nigeria.

A Proud Profession Gone Forever

The other day while I was clearing out papers from my home in the UK I came across a plan of a building. I couldn't read it well and thought it was a plan of the flat I've just sold, but my neighbour looked closely at it and read Boys Quarters! Of course I knew straight away that it had nothing to do with the UK and must be Nigeria. My neighbour had never heard of boys' quarters before as no such thing exists in the UK.

In Nigeria during the colonial period the expatriates lived in a separate part of the towns known as the Government Reservation Areas (GRA) in houses built by the companies and the ministries they worked for. The boys' quarters were rooms built behind the main house to accommodate their household staff comprising cooks, stewards, small boys and drivers. Today the term "boys' quarters" sounds so derogatory, but at the time the workers who lived in them were proud to be working in the household of an expatriate.

Once my husband and I visited a good friend of my father-in-law in the Kent area of England who had lived in Nigeria in the 30s to the 50s and there, in a place of honour in his farm house, was a painting of his former Hausa cook. This English family had paid for the education of the cook's family and had even sponsored their cook's pilgrimage to Mecca by road. Such generosity towards domestic staff was not unusual in those days. Unfortunately once the old dedicated expatriates left and Nigerians took over their positions, Hausa cooks were no longer in demand. Since, unlike the practice with expatriate employees, the companies and ministries that employed Nigerians were not responsible for the salaries of domestic staff.

We did on two occasions employ Northern cooks but they were not only responsible for cooking but also for washing and cleaning the home. They were very experienced in cooking European foods as they had worked for many expatriates in the past. I remember especially a specialty of ox tongue, cooked and sliced and pickled. I think this was inherited from some German family. Over the years I taught them how to prepare English food like dumplings (made with flour and suet), suet steam puddings and many cakes and sponges without using margarine. Lemon meringue was a favourite made from a tin of Blue Cross condensed milk and squeezed lemons. It's a great pity that the profession of dedicated Hausa cooks is no more. Gone and lost forever.

Astrid Clarke

I remember the years when there were many more expatriates living in Nigeria than now. At one time virtually every expatriate home in Nigeria had a Hausa cook who could prepare any English dish one would desire and who would serve with efficiency and pride. "Baba" could handle everything from dinner parties to ladies' teas to after school snacks for the children. If they didn't personally perform other household tasks like washing and ironing themselves, they could be relied upon to supervise junior workers and ensure the household ran smoothly. Theirs was a proud profession.

But over the years many of the expatriates were gradually replaced by Nigerians. And when they left, Baba was left behind. Very few Nigerians wanted to employ a Hausa cook since they usually had a relation or two living with them to help. Some were fortunate to obtain work in restaurants and clubs catering for expatriates but many were left unemployed.

Once when I found myself without domestic help, an old Baba applied to work for us. He must have hoped that since I was an expatriate his work would be similar to that he was used to. He started work with us with high expectations and I was happy to have someone who had worked for expatriates and would share my expectations for cleanliness and efficiency. But after only a few days he began to realize that our home was not what he had expected. Fortunately my sister-in-law who had grown up in Kano was staying with us at that time and she encouraged him to adjust to our way of life, even if it was not what he was used to. It was her presence that kept him coming to work that first week. But the next week he discovered that I expected him to iron the clothes on a table. To him this was intolerable. He solved the problem himself however. He had an ironing board that a former employer had left behind for him and he decided to bring it to our house. So he happily ironed all our clothes

39

on his ironing board instead of the table.

He struggled on for a few more days trying his best to please us. But a crisis came when, I asked him to prepare egusi soup. To him that was a big insult. He told me that cooking Nigerian soups was a woman's work and he didn't come to our house to do woman's work. Then he left our house in frustration and anger, without even collecting his ironing board.

I still use the ironing board and am reminded of all the proud elderly Hausa cooks and stewards who must have gone back to their villages where their wife cooks the soups for them.

Joanne Umolu

Wife Number One

Veronica Agwunobi

The rain has been torrentially pouring down after months of beautiful sunny weather as though it knows the thoughts I am about to evoke. I am here in London, now a widow, a grandmother, with five successful children all with their own families. Life, in general, has been good to me, having even survived the worldwide pandemic with my two weeks of Covid-19. Since leaving Nigeria, I have worked hard, climbing the ladder in both forensic mental health and learning disabilities and loving my varied job.

On the day I left Nigeria to return home to the UK, I was fifty-three years of age, and had been married for thirty-five years. I had, at the time, no idea how I was going to manage; I was leaving the man and others I loved behind, only taking my remaining child and a bag. I was afraid I had left it too late to start again, my certificates all lost with only experiences to my advantage. Having always said, if it happened, I would leave, and I left.

Initially, on arriving in London we boarded in a single-roomed accommodation. It was the roof over our heads, my daughter and myself, sleeping on a single bed together. It was our home, as we arrived back during the snowy nights. My young daughter, returning from her school, and I from my work. I knew I had a difficult job ahead of me to survive this traumatic time with both of us missing

Nigeria, Emeka my husband, our friends, and the family. My first pay packet paid for bedding and warm clothes from the nearby charity shop, costing next to nothing. The Oxfam shop, which almost gave away electrical goods at the time, sold me an unbelievably cheap second-hand TV, for our entertainment, and the second month I bought a tape recorder and a fridge from them. Feeling we had all our basic needs, every day we jumped onto that warm single bed, to watch the TV and eat the delicacies I had not eaten for years.

To keep us going mentally, every Sunday we went on day outings, climbing onto different numbered local buses, not knowing where we were going, with our A to Z in hand in case of getting lost. Sometimes going only to the bus terminal and coming back. Other times, something caught our eye, and off the bus we would jump, allowing us to experience unexpected adventures. Examples being the dangerously swinging Millennium Bridge on the second day of opening, before closing for repairs. Another, ice-skating on an open ice-rink and breaking my rib after getting onto the dodgem cars at a carnival, due to someone driving into the side of our car and my having to go to A&E.

Months later obtaining a job as a care manager, our accommodation improved, now affording a double room with a double bed, near my daughter's school, I started studying. Those were difficult, exhausting times, typing late into the early morning hours, thoughts of my young daughter's future keeping me going. All my children giving me moral and financial support for the education of their sister, with my senior daughter also supporting in the tutoring, resulting in her going to university. My career taking off and eventually becoming a manager of a twenty-eight bedded Mental Health Residential Care Home and later working in Forensic Mental health Supported Living after which, becoming an Executive Manager and overseeing multiple units, some catering for Learning Disabilities and Autism

My journey started in 1963; I was so excited. I was going to my first Student Union dance that night, with my old school friend Eddie. We had agreed to go to the dance together, as we were both new in Dundee, and fresh out of school. It was to be a special dance with a West Indian Steel Band invited to play. As we arrived the steel band was in full swing, the sound was electrifying, and the singing did not let us down either. As we stood side by side surveying the scene, I noticed the room was extremely basic, the wooden floorboards were grey with age and there were simple wooden chairs that surrounded the room for those requiring rest to sit on.

That was when he walked in, and I was instantly captivated by his dark eyes, and the smartness of his white shirt and tailored blue suit, with turned-up cuffs with buttons. I turned to Eddie and said, "Do you see him over there? I like him". My fate was almost sealed when later in the night we danced. We met two weeks later at another student dance, where we had gone looking for each other, and from that day on there was no going back, we were meant to be.

One day, when I had gone to visit Emeka at his home behind the University where he was studying, he said he wanted to show me something, he rummaged through a box in his cupboard and retrieved three photos. The first he showed me was of a seated young Nigerian woman, dressed up in a wedding dress, with Emeka standing behind with his hand rested on her shoulder. It looked like a wedding photograph. He informed me that this was one of his father's wives, that he was not married, and that before coming to the UK for his studies his father had insisted, he gets married. As Emeka had refused, the next best thing was this photograph, staged to ensure he could produce it and say he was already married. Emeka explained that he had been afraid that I might come across this photo and misunderstand.

He then showed me a photograph of his mother, showing a definite likeness to him. The third was a group photo with Emeka sitting in the middle, dressed in a suit, the only adult in the photo, surrounded by about thirty or more primary school-aged children and younger children, all in rows. I asked, in my ignorance, what primary school was it? Only to be informed, it was not a primary school and that these were his brothers and sisters. This was my first introduction to polygamy and that day Emeka started my education on the subject.

The story, my then-partner told me, was that my then future father-in-law (Papa), a successful self-made businessperson and a strong believer in the Catholic faith, in the 1950s had built a church in the village using his own money, for the priests to hold mass and be involved with the community. After being this practicing Catholic and one of the strongest pillars in the church for eleven years, Papa who had only had one child within the eleven years, and wanting more children, decided to take on a traditional wife, with several more following.

The church and the members became upset, and Papa was informed, by the priests he could no longer receive Holy Communion with the ultimatum that he should no longer have his concubines living under his roof if he ever wanted to be accepted back into the church. Papa's new dilemma was that these wives, all now with children existed, and he had responsibilities. In the hope it would solve his problem, he went over the road from his family compound and built another compound for these wives, where each wife was given a self-contained house of their own where they now happily resided. His first wife (Mama) had a large house built for her use within his compound.

Papa then went to the priests and told them he had moved his wives out, informing them, they no longer lived in his house in his compound. The priests refused this saying he was still having children with his wives, was living in sin, and would not be able to receive communion. This fractured relationship with the church was to continue throughout his life, where he could hear mass, but not take the sacraments. Although this was the situation, all his wives, and children went to church, as did their children, making up a large part of the congregation.

Time passed with rumblings of a pending Civil War in Nigeria, Emeka's father had sent an urgent letter saying the risk of the civil war was becoming closer and inevitable, and that he desperately needed the equivalent of £9.000 in today's currency, as he had taken out a loan on his hotel and was unable to repay it, with the lender very happy, as he wanted the hotel. The deadline date for payment given his father was pleading for help. We had no money left and were living hand to mouth as it was. Emeka knowing if money were not obtained from his bank the family would starve, went to Barclay's bank, spoke with the manager, obtained the precious loan, and immediately sent it to his father through the bank. It arrived half an hour before the debt collection was to happen, this was a great disappointment to the lender, the hotel being in a prize position of the town, and the man had wanted it. The situation saved, and the hotel continued to keep the family alive during the harsh civil war years which started in 1966 with a Military Coup d'état, orchestrated by General Ironsi, overthrowing the First Republic, and resulting in the Biafran War, seriously affecting the Igbo area Emeka's family came from.

My wedding day, at St Andrew's Church, in Dundee Scotland

arrived, with an agreement that Emeka would never take on a second wife and I would not stay if he did. It was his habit to appear a half-hour late on all occasions, but on that day I thought, he was leaving me at the altar. He and his best man eventually arrived. The priest quickly ushered him into the sacristy for a private word. He explained that an urgent telegram had arrived from his father who was trying to stop the wedding from ever taking place. It had been perfectly timed. Nevertheless the wedding did take place, with my husband sighing heavily beside me. I felt very confused, as I did not know what was going on.

My parents had unexpectedly appeared for the wedding, which surprised me, as my father had refused to meet him, offering me a world cruise. Followed by a business of my choice if I would change my mind. I was banned from Edinburgh, when I refused the offer, with the agreement to promise I would not let my siblings know I was getting married. My mother, on the other hand, who was a very practical woman had talked him into coming to our wedding, saying he would regret it if he did not come. Later, we all went for a meal together and that is where I learned that Papa had pleaded in his telegraph for Emeka not to marry me, as he had claimed it would kill him if Emeka went through with this marriage. Some years later, a very embarrassed Papa was to say he was sorry, he did regret what he had done, and I had ignored it anyway.

My official education into the different lifestyle I was going into was when I went to the Registry Office in Scotland to apply for a wedding license. The serious-faced gentleman told me it was his duty to inform me that men from countries like Nigeria could marry four or more wives and asked if I understood. To which, all of us who took this pathway in the sixties said we did, even if we did not have a clue.

Subsequently, in the sixties, once we were married out of our culture we followed our husband. And that was how it happened that twelve years later, in September 1974, I arrived with my four children in Jos, Plateau State, Nigeria where my husband had started a new job.

After a settling-in period, we travelled south to Onitsha, where introductions would be made. The family lived in Onitsha during the week and spent the weekends in their nearby village. At that time my Nigerian family had increased to nine wives and sixty-five children!! When we got to Onitsha we went to Papa's house where I was introduced to my mother –in –law. This meeting got off to a bad start with my mother-in-law upset and leaving the room we were all in. My husband informed me it was because my normal attire of jeans had upset Mama as she believed women who wore jeans were associated with armed robbers, as they could climb and run. I immediately changed into a skirt, Mama appeared back, and from that day on, we had a good understanding and relationship.

On Emeka's previous visit his mother had brought young women for him to choose from as she then believed he needed a Nigerian wife. He had refused and after meeting me, Mama had gone back to him and told him he was right, that he did not need a Nigerian wife, that this one was good enough for him. Mama protected me, advised me, arranged all cultural requirements, paid my dues to the village women's groups and fines for not attending their meetings. The village women's association gave me the nickname, 'Electrique', the light that lights up wherever it goes. Although some people thought it was an insult, I did not. Whenever I heard "Electric" or "Electrique" called out, I loved it. Mama looked after me and my children, often standing up to other family members when they said things about me that were not true, and I loved her dearly. Mama ensured I knew where I was in the family hierarchy and what my status was within the family. Firstly, I had married into the family and was positioned before the wives who had married my father-in-law after I had married his son, meaning I was before them in the line. I was also the first wife of the first son of Papa's first wife, which meant that I was recognised as someone who held a prominent position within the family. On special occasions, materials were allocated to the various groups in the family and uniforms were sewn. I would wear my allocated uniform along with the others in the same group. This was for identification as to what group each person belonged to in the family, such as Papa's wives, the wives of the sons, the sons, the married daughters, the teenage daughters, and the younger family members.

After meeting the family in Onitsha we drove to the family compound in the village. It was situated deep in the green valley and the sight that we saw driving down the steep hill, fighting with the deep ridges in the sandy road and the line of palm trees on the horizon was amazing. A diverse collection of people had come to meet this brother they had not seen for seventeen years and was now back in their midst with his Scottish wife and children. This caused great interest within the family and extended members. Emeka was allocated a large flat for us within the main house. . A senior wife had been chosen during his previous visit to support Emeka, to cook for him and to introduce him to chiefs and other visitors who were expected and to keep him safe.

Franca, a brother's wife, was assigned to take me around and to ensure the family's needs were satisfied. I visited his mother's house in the main compound before being taken over the road to the wives' compound and introduced to all the wives and their children (including the wife in the wedding photo) in their homes. They all made me very welcome.

Over the years Franca invested work and effort into the job she that had been delegated to her as we visited the surrounding extended families to give condolences or congratulations. It was a secure village lifestyle, even with family arguments, politics, and at times antagonism that I tried to keep out of and there was security in numbers

Back in Jos, life went on as we set up our family home, with my husband working in the University, and me supporting his businesses, taking care of my children and their schooling, making friends, sometimes painting, and enjoying my new life.

In December 1983, President Shagari was overthrown in a Coup d'état, and we entered the Buhari Regime with his War against Indiscipline, and its crackdown on corruption in Nigeria. There were executions: its cruelty shocking me.

At one point I joined Nigerwives, eventually becoming a National President, and travelling to attend our annual national meetings where we met old and new friends.

Throughout all there was the traditional side with my family, Emeka's chieftaincy and with the traditions becoming more intense as his father's physical health deteriorated resulting in his death,

Papa's funeral was one of the last of the old regimes with fortunes spent on lavish celebration to ensure his right of passage into the next world went smoothly. His body was embalmed, kept in the mortuary, and checked out regularly to ensure his wake would happen. The family arranged to have photos of the different family groups for a souvenir calendar. I had joined the wives for their group photo and was asked to move into the middle of the group, even although I objected. There I was, the only white face, in the middle, at the front, looking like something out of the colonial days, and squirming at the thought and knowing I would go down in history looking just like that.

In preparation for the funeral the family had organized heavy machinery to make the sandy road to the village drivable and to create a large car park for the large numbers expected. The hotel bands played for three days in both compounds, with different traditional ceremonies going on for the month. The married daughters each brought a cow for the occasion and arranged a dance troupe from their husband's village to dance at the celebrations. Guns were banned to avoid accidents, but gunpowder was set off as salutes. Cooks managed the eating arrangements for different visitors. There was great anxiety over the possibility of clashes between the Women's Christian Association and the prostitutes from Papa's hotel if they attended funeral events at the same time so the timing was carefully planned. Food and drinks were in abundance, with food for the chiefs cooked specially by the village women who came to support the family. Varied materials were arranged for everyone involved and suitable uniform outfits were sewn. I was to help in welcoming and serving the visiting chiefs their food and drink in the relaxed atmosphere of our flat. The wake was a success, the wives were traditionally prepared and on show in a room, crying for all to see, and were issued condolences in the passing. Dry hankies were secretly kept wet with the help of the outside tap in the yard to support in their tearful grieving which was difficult since it had been three months since Papa died.

The family had arranged an early morning family mass at church, which everyone attended. A car with the Papa's body drove past the church but was not allowed inside. The catechist arrived at the burial saying prayers over the body as it was laid to rest.

The burial celebrations went on for days. Papa's first daughter went around calling out his name throughout. I joined the women's circle dance. The dance troupes were magnificent. There was one group of men dressed in white wigs and painted faces who danced while carrying machetes that they clashed together. This caused me considerable anxiety until one dancer came forward and gently told me not to worry. At one point the funeral celebration reached a crescendo, the music was heady, a badly behaved bull broke free and chaos broke out with people running all over the place and dust flying everywhere, before the bull was caught, and secured.

Years passed. Then Emeka started to drop hints, like "I met a lawyer today who told me he has a wife in the village to look after his village house. He doesn't need to send her much money and only sees her every six months."

If we went somewhere he might say, "Look at that old man over there with that young wife. He has married her to look after him in his old age. That is what they do!"

This went on as he continued trying one ploy after another until early one morning he openly broached the subject, telling me what he wanted to do and what type of woman he would look for. Although he denied he had already found a woman to marry, I knew he had.

I went to his mother, who was not well at the time, to talk with her about her son wanting to take on another wife. She asked me how I felt about it and I told her I did not agree with it. She said if I did not want it, she would not agree. Then she told me how Papa had approached her about marrying another wife. He came so often that she gave up protesting and agreed although that was when all her problems had started.

Eventually, it did happen, with Emeka working extremely hard at it. He chose a young girl from a larger traditional family than our own, saying it was security for our properties and that it ensured he had support as his children were all abroad. My objections just went in one ear and out the other. He expected that I would eventually accept it as "the right thing to do." But I knew I would have to leave to look after myself. I had always said I would leave him if it happened and my children wholeheartedly supported me.

I decided I would go to the traditional wedding to see it done properly. My expatriate friends could not understand why I would even want to see it take place. They thought I was so calm because I was in shock. But for me, it was tying up the ends and not causing the family offense. It was important for me to do it properly as one never knows tomorrow, and even when I missed our times together, when there was no winner, and no going back; I would not feel guilty.

So I appeared calm but I felt hurt. More than that I was sad that 35 years of marriage and working together has finished like this. It hurt that an intruder had come to the cuckoo's nest and he was happily tucking her in.

I went to my Nigerian work team with many questions: If your husband took on another wife, what would you do? What happens during the ceremonies? What are the expectations on the first night? Would the husband sleep with his new wife or the old one? How does the old wife react on that night?

I was surprised at the answer. In Igbo culture if a man takes a new wife after multiple years of marriage, it is the man's fault and not the wife's fault. If it had been the wife's fault, he would have either thrown her out or taken another wife much sooner. Therefore he should sleep with his first wife on the night to show his respect.

I recall what happened when I went to talk with my husband and asked him which of us he was going to sleep with on the night? He nearly choked over his drink, as it went flying down his clothes. Stuttering, he told me I was not meant to ask questions like this! I reminded him that he had earlier told me there was no love between them and that they were having arguments already. Intending to sweeten any bitterness, he had said he was only doing this for some practical reasons. But I had wanted to know what was happening. I wanted to know where I was sleeping on the night. What was the arrangement? He replied that she was expecting to sleep with him and she would not be happy if he didn't since it was her wedding night after all.

I had sat looking at him intensely, waiting quietly, feeling like a stalking cougar, watching its prey in silence. In for the kill I said, "And…?" He had coughed knowing my quietness was not a good sign. He continued uncomfortably to admit that according to traditions he should sleep with me. I remember getting up from my chair and saying "Fine! If the traditions say that, then that is what is going to happen! We are sleeping together on the night". And I left the room with him in shock.

They had requested my photograph, being the first wife, for inclusion in the wedding calendar. But the photo was discarded later, not wanted, and that is when I realized the politics and fight were on. My uniform, a little more than a yard of material, arrived, and I was told I could make a dress, which to me was an insult as it was a traditional wedding and there was not enough material for anything but a very short, sleeveless, skimpy dress. I was not going to be remembered after 35 years, as the wife who turned up at this traditional wedding out of place in a skimpy dress. So I mustered up a friendly Igbo worker of mine and down to the market we went intending to ensure I was not disgraced. We bought a suitable top and picked out the shiniest gold stole to drape across my shoulder. A strip of material was put aside for my headband, which my friendly worker made up with a rose of the same material. I sewed large beads to the wrap around and to the rose, to give a little bit more 'Oomph,' and I already had a suitable necklace and shoes. The outfit was complete, and I was ready to follow the traditions as a first wife with some decorum and as much grace as possible, even if I was on my way out.

The wedding day arrived. I travelled to Anambra to the village with my Nigerwife friend, Kanchana. She did not look at the situation the same way I did. Her interest was to observe the occasion, but her presence was a great support for me. The celebrations were held in the wife's village in her family compound, with the young bride, whom I had met once, appearing with her entourage, wearing her lovely outfit, and myself sitting beside my husband looking the part. The music played, chiefs came and went, and drinks were flowing. Midway I started drowning my sorrows with beer and Kanchana was supportively beside me throughout. I had to get up to dance with my husband and 'my new wife' to show solidarity, which did not last long as I just looked out of place. As Emeka became upset at one point in the ceremony, I patted his hand which was next to me, encouraging him to calm down. Suddenly a figure dashed across the compound, and 'the wife' also patted his hand. Another time I leaned forward to speak to him quietly about something that was happening, and she appeared again, leaning over to talk in his ear. I knew without doubt polygamy was not for me.

We all drove back to our village compound in the family bus, with the wedding Mercedes abandoned due to the warning that there were armed robbers somewhere on the road awaiting the wedding party who would have money on them. Emeka spent the journey telling her he would be spending the night with me. She then wanted to go back to her mother's house, which in Igbo culture is not acceptable. On reaching our house, all of us tired and rooms allocated, when it came to bedtime I announced it was time to go to bed saying. "Ok Emeka, time for bed! Let's go!" And off to our bed, we went. I slept like a baby with my third eye open; he was not so rested.

In the morning when we got up, he rushed out to see her. I then discovered she had slept on the couch overnight, which meant if I had not slept in my bed, which she had intended to sleep on, I would have been the one on the couch. Any feelings of guilt or pity disappeared. This was salt to the wound even if the couch was comfortable. Later she came to me saying she had made a mistake and she should have talked with me. I agreed, realizing she was as much a victim in this as I was.

On returning to Jos, I had no doubts about what I was going to do. I cleared out my house, divided our family photographs, headed off to Kano as fast as possible with my daughter and a bag. I was ready to join the rest of my children and my new life ... with apprehension and not knowing what was ahead, but ready to embrace it.

Fishy Tales

I am from Jamaica and grew up very fond of the many varieties of sea fish which were readily available on our island nation. I had recently arrived in Nigeria and joined my husband, Simeon, in Oshogbo, a city many miles inland.

One morning at breakfast Simeon asked me if I liked fresh fish. "Oh yes", I replied eagerly. He said he would buy me some later in the day. He left for work shortly afterwards and I began my daily routine of putting away dishes and cleaning up. We had not yet gotten a steward to help around the house.

At about 11 am Simeon drove in and after parking the car by the front door he came in with a big plastic bucket. I hurriedly opened the door for him and he stood before me beaming. He held out the bucket to me saying, 'Here's your fish!' I was about to take it from him when I noticed about three long black fish swimming around in the bucket. I walked away from the door in shock. He apparently did not notice my reaction because he went straight into the kitchen, filled up the kitchen sink with water and put the fish in where they continued swimming around.

He then took the bucket and strode out of the house telling me to please put lots of hot pepper when seasoning the fish. He promised to be back early for dinner.

I can't imagine how he didn't notice the shock on my face or my lack of response. He drove off and I burst into tears. "What am I doing? What have I gotten myself into? "I had no idea I would be expected to kill the fish I would prepare for dinner. When he asked me earlier if I liked fresh fish I didn't know he meant 'live' fish!

I had a horrible day. I did not go to the kitchen even once because the kitchen sink was right at the door leading from the dining room to the kitchen area. I had no intention of passing those living, swimming, snake-looking fish!

Needless to say no dinner was prepared that day.

When my husband arrived home that evening I hid in the garden. I heard him calling me but I didn't respond. He found his dinner still swimming in the kitchen sink. He started looking all over for me. I finally emerged from my hiding place behind a car in the yard. I told him I liked fresh fish, not live fish! He burst into laughter and told me not to worry, he would cook dinner.

I must tell you he didn't know how to kill the fish either! He called the security guard at the gate and asked him to kill the fish. That's something I didn't think of. He then made dinner, but I didn't eat. I had lost my appetite.

Needless to say he never brought me fresh or live fish again.

Joan Iheukumere

What I saw on my kitchen sideboard and which sent me into a fit wasn't fresh fish but a monitor lizard! A bloody specimen freshly killed and purchased on the road was left in my kitchen by my brother-in-law. He had arrived after a long interstate road journey and had purchased this piece as a gift for his mother who happened to be in our home. I fled from the kitchen on seeing it and refused to go in until the creature was removed and my kitchen sanitized. Having grown up a vegetarian, I had made huge strides in the culinary department on coming to Nigeria. Over the years I learned to cook chicken, beef and goat meat. But it ended there. My husband bought me a coffee table-cook book which made cutting a chicken into segments seem like an artistic enterprise. Bush meat was discreetly hidden in the freezer and cooked by the relatives. My husband insisted that the monitor lizard be taken to the backyard out of sight, where it was turned into pepper soup over a wood fire and suitably relished by the extended family.

My friend Sulekha spoke with passion of buying goat meat and packaging it. It was embarrassing. She selected the goat, male or

54

female, bought it, brought it home, cut, and washed it lovingly piece by piece. She said she then sat down and admired it on the colander before packaging it for the freezer. A meal was not a meal if it didn't have meat in it. The more the beef or chicken in the stew, the more festive the meal became.

Kanchana Ugbabe

When we lived in Port Harcourt in the mid-1960s I had a friend who loved Efik food and she enjoyed introducing me to various traditional dishes. One day she came to our house to teach me how to prepare her favourite soup. We had all the ingredients ready except for periwinkles, which she had sent someone to the market to buy for us. So we started cooking the soup and it looked delicious. I was eagerly looking forward to adding the pretty periwinkle flowers when they arrived. Before long there was a knock on the door and when my friend opened it I heard her exclaim 'Ah, these are beautiful periwinkles.' I looked expectantly at what she was proudly holding only to discover that the beautiful periwinkles were not flowers but snails – live snails! Trying to hide my shock, I stammered out, 'Oh, I've never seen these before!' I left the rest of the preparation to my friend, discretely keeping a distance between me and the cooking pot. Needless to say, I didn't have the courage to taste my friend's favourite soup. And I still don't know how periwinkle flowers would taste in soup either.

Joanne Umolu

Transplanted

Joanne Umolu

I grew up in a small farming community in Wisconsin, USA. Everybody looked alike, talked alike and had little or no interest in life beyond their community. However, although my widowed mother had never lived outside Wisconsin, she had a keen interest in other cultures. She sponsored children from different countries through a Save the Children organization and shared with my brother and me her enthusiasm for the children and the countries they lived in. It was during a family holiday visit to New York that a latent desire to interact with people from other countries was awakened. When our guided tour of New York City took us to the United Nations building I was suddenly in a thrilling international environment. Seeing the extent of my enthusiasm my mother arranged for us to leave the guided tour the next day so we could return to the United Nations building for a second visit. Although I didn't know it at the time, this was a sign of a zeal for international experiences that characterised my entire life. Certainly, I now credit my mother for recognising and supporting my cross cultural interests then and beyond.

My first experience of living abroad was when I travelled to Germany under a work abroad programme for university students. With my mother's blessing, I travelled alone to Germany where I had the opportunity to interact with people from many parts of the world who were working and studying in Germany. It was there I met an engineering student who later became my husband and eventually took me to his home country, Nigeria. Thus, I became an American transplanted in Nigeria, the country where I put down roots and grew to love.

I first set foot in Nigeria in 1965 when I travelled to join my husband, Joe, with our three year old son, Chukwuma, and baby daughter, Ifeoma, who was born just seven weeks earlier in the USA. Joe had taken up employment as an engineer with an Italian company constructing Kainji Dam, the first hydroelectric dam in Nigeria located in what was then the Northern Region. So my first experience of life in Nigeria was in a work camp built for the Italian, British, Dutch and Nigerian workers

My encounter with a custom that was to be a part of my life throughout all my years in Nigeria took place the day Joe brought the children and me to the house that had been allocated to him in the staff quarters of the Kainji construction camp. It was a small, newly constructed two bedroom bungalow. When we entered the house, we were welcomed by about ten young boys, Joe's junior brothers and cousins who were spending their school holidays with him in Kainji. Joe had often told me of the importance of extended family in Nigeria and the obligations involved and I was determined to accept this aspect of his culture. However, it was a shock to enter our house in Nigeria for the first time and find it filled up with young boys. They occupied the second bedroom which I had expected would be for our children. The single bathroom was always in use with water all over the floor. And I didn't feel free in the small kitchen where the boys cooked huge pots of food for themselves continually.

Fortunately, most of them left after the first week and I gradually began to get acquainted with those who stayed on and I felt a bit freer in my new home. Over the years Joe's family became my family. Those young boys later married and had children, many of whom I raised in our home. They are now grandfathers and their grandchildren are now my very precious grand nieces and nephews.

I had only lived in Kainji for one year when we were forced to flee under very tragic circumstances. In January 1966 there was a military coup d'état followed by a counter coup in July. These coups involved military officers of the three main ethnic groups, Hausa, Igbo and

Yoruba. The Hausas lived in the Northern Region which is where the dam site was located while the Eastern Region was made up mainly of Igbos and the Western Region was the home of the Yorubas. Many of the workers on the Kainji dam were Igbos and Yorubas, as well as people from other ethnic groups who had left their homes in the South and were living in the Kainji work camp. The coup and counter coup heightened ethnic tensions throughout the country, including the Kainji Dam site. Anti-Igbo sentiment grew in the Northern Region and many Igbos who worked on the dam anticipated violent attacks against them and returned to their native villages in the Eastern Region.

My husband, Joe, is Igbo and he was one of the most senior engineering staff working on the construction of the dam. We had decided not to leave Kainji, hoping the sentiment against the Igbos living in the Northern Region would not escalate. And so, we were still there on September 28, 1966, when Hausas began to attack Igbos living and working in the Northern Region. The night of September 28, some Igbo workers were attacked in Kainji in what appeared to be developing into a massive attack on Igbos the following night.

Suddenly it became imperative for us to flee Kainji and I began packing as much as I could in a few suitcases while Joe desperately tried to make arrangements for us to escape Kainji before nightfall. Our fears were intensified when we learned of a plan to target Joe, he being the most senior Igbo working on the dam, to be among those to be killed that night along with all the junior Igbo workers.

Joe was desperate to meet the Italian officials of his company to arrange for us to fly to Lagos on the daily company flight, but we were told they were in an emergency meeting. We were standing outside our house with our three suitcases when we heard the sound of an airplane. We looked up and our hearts sank. The plane was flying out of Kainji without us. Now we had no choice but to spend the night in Kainji. But where could we be safe? We were still standing outside when we got the news that the Italian company had arranged for all the families of the senior staff to spend the night in the school for Italian workers' children where we were assured there would be special security. So, we locked our house and drove in our red VW beetle to the school.

One of the many beds set up in one of the classrooms was allocated to our family. The atmosphere among the Italian families was as if they were having a picnic as they laughed and joked and enjoyed the food they had brought. Our mood was very different. We knew we were in danger. We knew we could never return to our home and we had not even thought of packing food to eat. Since Joe knew he had been targeted for an attack that night he began considering where else he could spend the night where it would be safer. It occurred to us that it was too risky to leave our bright red beetle in the school as it would reveal his presence there. So we came up with a plan for me to drive the car to a place where it could be hidden and also make a quick trip back to our house to release our dog that we had locked up in the kitchen. I left my family and took off in our red VW. It was getting dark when I reached the road to our house. Terrible shouting and screaming could be heard coming from the direction of the junior camp as if people were being pursued and were running for their life. I turned around in a panic and headed back toward the senior camp and the school room. Along the way I found a place just off the road where there were trees and tall bush and I hid the car there. Then I took off on foot toward the school. It was now almost dark. One of my shoes had lost a strap so I was struggling to run down the road as fast as I could barefooted when an expatriate family, also heading to the school saw me and gave me a lift.

The children and I spent the night on the bed in the classroom, but my husband didn't feel safe enough to stay with us. Instead, he climbed a tree in the school compound and that is where he spent the night. Morning came and the Italian families cheerfully packed up to go back to their homes. Soon Joe and I and our children were left alone and we began to panic. Where could we go and be safe? To our great relief, an English man drove by in a jeep and saw us. He told us that many workers had been killed during the night, and he had spent the night carrying the wounded to the hospital. When we told him of our fears for our safety, he took us to an office with a strong lock for us to wait in and phoned the Italian officials to tell them where we were hiding.

What a relief when a bus with an Italian driver, escorted by two soldiers with rifles who had been brought in during the night, arrived to pick us. The windows of the bus were covered with closed curtains so we could remain hidden. I was terrified when Joe pulled back a curtain and began to take photographs of the crowds of wounded workers waiting along the road side to be taken to a city further south for safety. At last, we reached the airstrip and got on the small piper cub heading to Lagos.

As we left, we were certain we would never set foot in the Northern Region again. Little did we know then that we would eventually make our home in northern Nigeria.

Like the hundreds of survivors of the pogrom who fled to their ancestral villages in Eastern Nigeria, we made our way to my husband's home town, Obosi, located near Onitsha. Virtually every Igbo family had at least one relation living in the Northern part of Nigeria where the massacres of the Igbos had taken place. Like villagers throughout the Eastern Region, everyone in Obosi had been anxiously waiting and watching for any surviving family members to arrive home.

At last we reached Obosi, exhausted from our sleepless two-day journey from Lagos. All our belongings were in the luggage we had tied to the roof of our car and were now drenched from the rain along the way. I was feeling quite nervous about meeting my husband's relations in the village for the first time. But I could never have imagined the reception we were about to receive.

It began as we were driving through the village to the family compound and we met several groups of women walking along the road. The women recognised Joe and immediately began shouting and dancing for joy as they came to the car to welcome us with warm embraces. Apparently they somehow spread the news of our arrival and by the time we finally reached the family compound what seemed like hundreds of people had already gathered to welcome us. Somehow in the midst of the dancing, clapping and embracing we managed to off-load our children and our wet luggage into the two very small rooms some family members had kindly vacated for us. The sounds of rejoicing continued well into the night while we struggled to get desperately needed sleep.

At about 5am people started gathering again in front of our house making so much noise it was impossible to sleep any longer. Suddenly we heard loud gunshots right outside the house. The children were frightened and thought people wanted to shoot us. However, the gun shots were to announce to the rest of the village an important event and to invite them to come to our compound. I wasn't even dressed when I was again meeting more hundreds of people.

I started to try to get the children dressed in any dry clothes I could find in our luggage. Some of the women followed me wherever I went and sat and watched as I tried to feed the children. Then suddenly one woman took off with Ifeoma and disappeared. It was Chukwuma who found her and excitedly came to show me where she was. I saw Ifeoma behind the big house in a pan of dirty water screaming her head off. A large crowd of adults and hundreds of little children were all watching her having her bath. A woman dried her in a filthy towel and I grabbed her and rushed back to our room as fast s as I could, while pretending to show I appreciated her help.

One of the women then told me to let her know when I wanted to have my bath. I didn't tell her, of course. Imagine me washing in front of ten million people! To my great relief, my husband's wonderful sister, Rose, came to my rescue and quietly took me to her husband's family home where I bathed privately. There I had a bucket bath outdoors, but within a small fenced in area open to the skies. How I enjoyed the luxury of having a few minutes all alone in a serene environment!

We had been in the village for less than a week when we were rescued again by Mary, another of my husband's wonderful sisters. Mary and her husband lived in the University town of Nsukka, which was about a three hour drive north of Obosi. With great relief, we relocated to Nsukka where we thoroughly enjoyed their small bungalow with a big yard for the children to run around in. I remember reassuring my mother that there was no more reason to worry about us, because now that we were in Nsukka we were "VIP" refugees. I didn't mention to her that my VIP life included the challenge of spending my days fetching buckets of water from down the road and trying to wash the notorious Nsukka red clay from the children's clothes. That problem was soon solved, however. Why dress the children in clothes when they can play outdoors under the Nsukka sun wearing just their underpants?

About a month later my husband was able to join an engineering company in Port Harcourt where we soon settled in comfortably. Port Harcourt was the most cosmopolitan town in the southern part of the Region. It would have been a very pleasant city to live in if there had not been the build up of tension between the Eastern Region and the Nigerian Government. In the aftermath of the September massacres of Igbos in the North and the return of Igbos from all over the country to the safety of their homeland, a movement to secede from Nigeria and form an independent nation called Biafra swiftly gathered momentum. The Nigerian Government anticipated this and blockaded the Eastern Region in order to prevent a military build up. We had been living in Port Harcourt for only a few months when we were no longer able to send or receive mail, thus cutting us off from our very worried families abroad. Imported food items and those normally brought from the north were no longer available. We prepared our meals without beef or fresh vegetables. I remember sifting weevils out of rancid flour whenever I was lucky enough to find any at all. So even before the war started, life was difficult and everyone had hopes that it would improve if Biafra could be an independent nation.

As the tension increased, expatriates living and working in Port Harcourt with Shell oil and other related companies left on evacuation flights. Eventuality those of us married to Igbo men were the only expatriate women left in Port Harcourt. In May 1967, the Eastern Region seceded and we suddenly lived in the independent nation of Biafra. Nigerian troops invaded Biafra on July 2, 1967, just three days after our daughter Ifeoma's second birthday. As we women moved around town, to avoid suspicion that we were foreign spies, we all dressed in local wrappers and demonstrated our solidarity with the Biafran cause by tying branches on the front of our cars. We soon discovered that if we always carried our children with us we could breeze through the numerous checkpoints and be spared the need to explain our presence in fledgling Biafra.

At first we were all confident that the war would be brief and we looked forward to enjoying life in an independent Biafra. But the Federal Government troops were more powerful and Biafra began to shrink in size as more and more Biafran territory was conquered. Soon after the war started, the engineering company where my husband worked was forced to close down and we no longer had an income. After a bomb was dropped on a field near the school Chukwuma attended, all the schools in Port Harcourt were closed. By October of 1967, the Federal Government troops were advancing toward Port Harcourt. There was no other option than for us to find a way to leave Biafra and travel to the USA where we could live until the war was over.

The next challenge was how to travel out of Biafra since it was impossible to go by road or air. However, some enterprising fishermen who lived in the Niger Delta and were very familiar with the delta creeks had started carrying passengers from Biafra to the Republic of Cameroon in canoes. Because of their intimate knowledge of the mangrove creeks in the delta they were able to establish a route which evaded the Federal Navy Ships stationed at the edge of the delta. When we learned that an old ferryboat had begun to carry a larger number of Biafran refugees through the delta creeks to the Cameroon Republic, we immediately prepared to travel.

So in late October 1967, we left everything behind in Port Harcourt except for what we could carry in a few suitcases and drove to the small port town of Oron, in what is now Awka Ibom State, to board the ferry. Thus began our journey as Biafran refugees.

At Oron, we boarded the old ferry boat crowded with men, women and children and managed to secure enough space on some wooden benches for the four of us and our three pieces of luggage. There we settled in for the journey through the creeks to the port town of Mamfe, in South West Cameroon which we were to reach sometime the following day. We travelled most of the day in what was still Biafran territory, nervously fearing that we would be caught by the Federal Navy boats stationed not far away. When night was about to fall the boat docked and passengers had the opportunity to climb up to a kiosk where food was served. Unfortunately, Ifeoma and I missed the meal since we needed to stay to make sure our luggage wasn't stolen while Joe and Chukwuma left to eat. Our plan to take our turn to eat when they returned ended in disappointment because the ferry took off again. This time it docked in a sheltered area that turned out to be near the Biafran border where we were to go through Biafran customs and immigration formalities. Up on a rock there was a table and some chairs occupied by Biafran immigration officers. Our passports were duly inspected and stamped and we were now ready to officially depart the Republic of Biafra. We marveled at the efficiency of the Biafran government in the midst of the war to ensure that such formalities were carried out even in obscure locations.

When we returned to the boat it docked in a nearby sheltered area to spend the night. We eagerly looked forward to the daylight as we waited, hungry and sleepless, on the hard benches. At last it was day break, and we soon took off on a fascinating adventure through the creeks toward the Cameroon Republic. If we had not been travelling as refugees we would surely have enjoyed the journey through mangrove swamps as we maneuvered through narrow creeks surrounded by bamboo trees. Turning and twisting, each section of a creek looked alike to us and we marveled that the pilot of our boat could know the way to go. The creeks were so narrow that, when we reached a place where a tree had fallen there was no room for us to pass. Our journey was held up until the crew came out with saws and axes to remove the tree and clear the way for us to pass through.

Finally in the late afternoon our boatload of Biafran refugees reached Mamfe. We eagerly disembarked, confident that we would soon be resting in a comfortable hotel. But that was not to be. We were first delayed by a group of international news reporters who had met the boat in order to get the latest news of the war and conditions in Biafra. We passed up that opportunity to tell the world about the suffering of the people of Biafra and made our way to the path leading to the Cameroonian customs and immigration offices. Struggling with our luggage and two exhausted and hungry children we trekked what seemed a very long distance to an open field where tents had been set up for immigration procedures and customs inspection. There we joined long queues waiting to enter various tents to go through seemingly endless immigration formalities, complicated by the fact than we had all arrived in Cameroon without a visa. The immigration officers were in no hurry and the customs officials took their time to go through every item of each passenger's luggage.

It seemed like hours later when we finally emerged with the necessary stamps in our passports. At long last we were able to get a taxi to take us to Kumba, a city about 150 Km away, where we could spend the night comfortably. Joining us in the taxi was another family who had traveled on the same ferry as us - a Biafran man with his American wife and small child. We planned that our two families would travel together to Kumba. In the morning we would take a taxi to Duala where there was an American Consulate prepared to repatriate US citizens fleeing the war in Biafra.

It was already dark when we entered Kumba. With great relief we checked into a hotel and walked down the road to eat in a nearby restaurant. On our way back to our hotel we heard loud music playing and wondered if there was a party going on in our hotel. We went straight to our room and prepared for the long awaited chance to sleep. Suddenly the music became much louder -- so loud it was impossible for us to sleep. When the music became unbearably loud Joe went out to complain to the hotel management. There he learned that the staff wanted to make us feel welcome, knowing we had just escaped from the war in Biafra. Not only had they decided to play music for us, but so that we would enjoy the music even more, they had moved the speakers as close to our room as possible!

The next morning we set off in a taxi for Duala -- two Biafran/Nigerian husbands, two American wives and three children. The distance from Kumba to Duala was only about 70km but as it turned out the journey was far from smooth. There were numerous police checkpoints along the way where our passports were meticulously examined to ensure we were travelling with requisite Cameroonian visa and permits. When all was found to be in order we were cleared to continue our journey. We were about to enter Duala when we met another checkpoint where we expected to have another routine check. However, when the police examined the passport of our Biafran travel companion they told him he didn't have the correct permit to travel in Cameroon. They said they were going to detain him in a police station in Duala, but the rest of us were free to continue to our destination.

We immediately went on to Duala and drove straight to the American Consulate where the distraught American wife hoped to get help in releasing her husband. There was no legal grounds for an American Consulate officer to pursue the release of a non-American citizen who held a Nigerian Passport with a Biafran exit stamp But to our great relief, immediately we reached the consulate and reported that the husband of the American was being detained by the police, one of the American Consular officers dashed out to secure his release.

In the coming days we observed more evidence of the dedication of the Consular staff who worked tirelessly to assist the numerous Americans who came to Duala as refugees from Biafra to apply for repatriation to the USA. The Consulate offices overflowed with Americans, some like us with non-citizen family members, who spent days there waiting to fly out. The Consulate obtained an American visa for my husband, who had never set foot in the USA. With financial assistance from my mother who had been in contact with the American consulates on our behalf even when we were still in Biafra, they also purchased our tickets and booked our flights to America. We had been in Duala for about a week when one of the officers in Consulate drove us personally to the international airport and we set off on our journey to the USA.

We lived, worked and studied in the USA for almost five years. We had settled into Columbus Ohio where Joe had a good job as an engineer. But while the war continued, his heart was always back in Biafra imagining the suffering of his family and friends there. The reports of the starvation of Biafran children had a profound effect on us. We formed an organisation called Friends of Biafra and worked tirelessly to create public awareness of the plight of the children in Biafra and to raise funds for them.

I had become deeply concerned about the effects of protein deficiency on Biafran children since it could result in brain damage. So I enrolled in Ohio State University to obtain a Master's degree in Special Education with the intention of returning to Biafra after the war to establish schools for children who had intellectual disabilities as a result of growing up with protein deficiency.

But in January 1970 everything changed. Nigeria won the war and there was no longer any Biafra to go back to. Nigeria, the country we never thought we would live in again, gradually drew us back. Soon we were eagerly preparing to return to live in Lagos where my husband had been offered a position with the Nigerian Electric Power Authority.

Joe was passionate about dams and was thrilled to have the opportunity to apply his engineering skills toward the development of hydroelectric dams in Nigeria. I looked forward to using my Special Education qualification to get a teaching job in Lagos.

When we returned from the USA in 1972 Chukwuma had finished 4th Grade and Ifeoma had finished 1st Grade. Chukwuma had lost the little Igbo he had acquired in Port Harcourt and had little memory of life in Biafra. Despite all our efforts to encourage them to identify with their father's culture while we were in Columbus, Chukwuma and Ifeoma arrived Lagos basically as Americans. At first they were enrolled in the American International School where I also was employed and most of their friends were expatriates. However, gradually they were impacted by Nigerian culture and began to feel comfortable in it. It helped them that there were almost always extended family members staying with us. They enjoyed our trips to other parts of the country, including visits to the now completed Kainji Dam where we had fled the massacres in 1966. By the time they attended Nigerian secondary schools they were quite comfortable moving back and forth between their American and Nigerian cultures.

The American influence became stronger for our two children in the late 1970s when the deterioration of the quality of secondary education in Nigeria forced us to seek alternatives. Chukwuma had been attending St. Gregory's College, the same school which his father had attended in the 1940s when it was one of the most outstanding secondary schools in Lagos. We reluctantly withdrew him just before his final year and sent him to stay with my brother in USA in order to prepare him for admission to an American university. Ifeoma was attending Holy Child College, the sister school of St. Gregory's College where I also taught until 1979 when we decided she also needed to change to a school with higher standards. That was what brought us to Jos, a city in the north central Nigeria, so Ifeoma could attend Hillcrest School, an excellent secondary school run by expatriate missionaries.

So it was in Jos, the capital city of Plateau State where we finally settled. When we had fled Kainji in 1966, we never imagined we would live in what was then the Northern Region where the massacre of the Igbos took place. And when we left

Biafra in 1967 we had no idea that we would ever live in a country called Nigeria again. It seems ironic that this city in North Central Nigeria is the very place where we have settled and lived happily for more than 40 years now. It is here I grew roots deep in the Nigerian soil as I was engaged in very fulfilling activities that would not have been possible if I still lived in the USA.

We purchased land, built a big house and kept it filled it up with children. I became "Big Aunty" in the Umolu family and my husband "Big Uncle" as over the years our home was the base for numerous nephews and nieces who came from other parts of Nigeria to attend school in Jos. Most of them have now grown up and have children of their own, so now I am still acquiring more "grandchildren".

It was in Jos that I had the opportunity to develop professionally and pursue my passion for teaching reading. During my 20 years as a lecturer in the Department of Special Education in the University of Jos, I was actively involved in the Reading Association of Nigeria, and at one point served as the National President. Over the years I represented Nigeria at numerous international conferences and also served as the head of the Africa Committee of the International Reading Association. The young girl who had been thrilled to visit the United Nations building was now happily involved in literacy development activities in an international and intercultural environment –an involvement made possible by my Nigerian background.

My roots grew deeper in Nigerian soil after I left the University and established Open Doors Special Education Centre on land my husband had purchased. Working directly with children with disabilities and their families required intense commitment to meeting their needs and a deeper involvement in the community. By including a Reading Clinic Unit in the Centre, I continued to pursue my passion for teaching children to read. Open Doors Special Education Centre now serves an average of 90 children and young people with learning and physical disabilities. I served as Director for twenty years and the Centre is now thriving under new leadership.

I am now semi-retired and largely confined to home. But my life is enriched by two young girls who we recently brought into our home at ages 9 and 14 years. Aside from the fun of being called "Mommy" again at an age when I am "Grandma" to much older children, I have thoroughly enjoyed making up for their lack of schooling with my Special Education background and passion for teaching children to read.

So here I am, born and raised in the USA but now transplanted in my Nigerian husband's country. Sometimes people ask me if I feel I am an American or a Nigerian. I tell them I feel like a Nigerwife. I am bicultural. My bicultural children are currently living in the USA with their Nigerian-American families. Even my mother, who visited Nigeria every two years until her death, became well known in our small Wisconsin town as a Nigeria enthusiast. As for my husband, he may be tilted culturally more on the Nigerian side. But then he can surprise me, like the other day when he said he was tired of Nigerian soups and instead I should give him German black bread with sliced ham and cheese!

From New Delhi to the Heart of Igboland

Agness Agomuo

I am from Kerala, India. I met Ebere, my Nigerian husband, through my roommate while I was studying nursing in New Delhi. We had agreed to be married, but without the knowledge of our family. So in December 1985 we made the two-day train journey to my hometown in the South-eastern State of Kerala to introduce my fiancé to my family. To our dismay my mom's first sight of him was such a shock to her that she literally fainted. She had never seen anyone before who was not Indian, and here I was bringing home an African. Fortunately, my family eventually supported our marriage which took place without hitches.

We left for Nigeria in November 1986. When we arrived in Lagos we stayed with my husband's elder brother and his family. I had to adjust quickly to living in overcrowded conditions. Their family of three adults and four children occupied a two- bedroom apartment. A common kitchen and a common bathroom was shared by more than eight families. The bathroom was the most difficult thing for me to adjust to. I also had to adjust to staying in Lagos without Ebere, as two days after our arrival he left for northern Nigeria for his compulsory service with the National Youth Service Corp.

It is the tradition in Nigeria for Igbos who live in different parts of the Country to travel back to their ancestral villages over Christmas. So after my two week stay in very uncomfortable conditions in Lagos, we all set out by bus to spend the Christmas period in my husband's village Ikem Nvosi in Abia State in Eastern Nigeria. We started our journey from Lagos in the early morning and arrived in the village around 6:30 pm just as it was getting dark. . I was exhausted from the long bus journey and felt nervous as we reached the family compound. There was no electricity and the family members who came to welcome us looked strange by the light of the lanterns some of them carried. Suddenly the women started making a loud, high pitched, rhythmic sound which I soon learned was used to inform neighbours that something special is happening in their compound. In just a few minutes many people came rushing in. To my great discomfort it turned out it was me, a strange "white" woman, they were invited to come and see. Using a lantern they inspected me from head to toe. I didn't understand what was happening. I felt miserable and alone as I experienced my first encounter with my husband's family in his village without him.

Gradually the visitors left us and I had the opportunity to meet the numerous family members. My father-in-law had two wives, the first wife being the mother of my husband, my husband's elder brother with whom we stayed in Lagos and four sisters. Also there were three step brothers and a step sister. I was given a room to stay in along with my husband's nine year old niece. Throughout the evening my father-in-law seemed very happy as he sat near me and held me close. He told everyone in the family that he never thought he would see an *oyinbo* with his eyes, and now here he was having one of his own. At last I was beginning to feel better and looked forward to a long night's sleep and even sleeping in late in the morning. But that was not to be. Very early in the morning before we woke up, my brother-in-law knocked on our door and asked me to get dressed and come out. I peeped through the window and saw many people in the compound. I also saw crates of soft drinks and packets of biscuits in front of my father-in-law's house. I became very frightened. I had heard from people in India that Africans ritually sacrifice human beings and I felt a sudden panic that they were getting ready to sacrifice me.

As I prepared to go out my brother-in-law advised me not to shake hands with anybody. I opened the door and saw a lot of people singing and dancing in jubilation. My father-in-law was saying something to them in their language which I didn't understand. I thought they are going to kill me any moment. But minutes went by and then hours went by and nothing happened to me. They did not kill me. The next day again nothing happened to me. Only people from other villages came to look at the *oyinbo*. I gradually got used to the stares of the women who followed me everywhere I went. I even learned to smile at the children who timidly came close to me to feel my hair. Finally, after fourteen days in the village without my husband, Ebere returned. We stayed another two weeks in the village during which I delighted in the new role he assumed as a graduate returnee from India and the proud husband of the renowned *oyinbo*.

Circles and Silver Threads

Kenna Owoh

When I reflect on my life as a Nigerwife - the wife of Aaron Chikwendu Owoh - and my ongoing fascination with 'things Nigerian', I tend not to think in terms of events on a chronological order – like beads on a string. Rather, I think of a Venn diagram – that diagrammatic logic tool of multiple, overlapping closed circles where each circle represents a set of variables that intersect in overlapping spaces. These intersections add yet more variables, more richness, layer upon layer. In my imagination those circles are the various geographic spaces in our life together, Aaron's and mine, where we were implanted for varying periods of time. Each circle with its own actors, structural imperatives, institutions, mores, and expectations is a space where Aaron and I acted and reacted, were shaped and reshaped, accrued experiences, grew individually and together, and purposely changed our lives. And we gathered together those changes, packing them up and carrying them with us to the next geographic space, to fill a new circle with shades of experiences. We – a Canadian woman with my Nigerian husband - moved about: from Canada to Scotland, to Zambia, back to Canada; to Nigeria, to Canada, back to Nigeria; and now in Canada. And throughout stopping in Europe, Middle East, other parts of Africa, and every region of Nigeria. I became consistently a Nigerwife, where Nigeria – in all its expressions – became part of my being. So, my story is a story of spaces – those circles of diverse shades making up a striking whole. And weaving throughout these circles are the *silver threads of family and friends* – but more about that later.

I am starting somewhere between Winnipeg and Toronto, Canada, 1966: I was travelling on the train after a visit to my parents in Winnipeg in central Canada, returning to Toronto where I was training to be a nurse. In those days the Canadian National passenger trains were largely serviced by 'black porters', polite young black men who made the beds, delivered drinks, provided information and generally serviced the passengers. This cadre was dominated by African and Caribbean university students working their summer jobs trying to accumulate sufficient funds to top up their scholarships. Aaron was one of those students. He had come to Toronto in 1965 after receiving a scholarship to Wilfred Laurier University in Kitchener with £5 in his pocket and a large suitcase full of hope. We talked; he was interesting; we agreed to meet again. This was my introduction to Nigeria. Over the next two years I met his Nigerian fellow students; was introduced to his circle of West Indian friends, learned about the ongoing Biafran War in which Aaron, an Igbo, was actively engaged. And my world was enlarged. Completely different from my white, traditionalist Canadian background. One of those friends – Peter, and his wife Elizabeth, both from Akwa Ibom – live near to me today – *a silver thread.* I heard Aaron's tales of racism, denial of accommodation, and snide comments that were made. How did I not know this? We respected and valued each other; thoughts of marriage and a life together followed. On completion of his BA in 1967 Aaron received a British Council scholarship for Aberdeen, Scotland and started further studies there. I completed my nursing in 1968 and received a scholarship to study midwifery in Aberdeen. In 1969 we married in Canada. My sister supported me. My father refused to 'give me away' – he believed he was acting on his principles – but principles can change, and he changed his after a time. We stepped into a new circle.

This was a cold circle – no central heating in North Sea impregnated, damp Aberdeen. Living in a basement flat, it was a shilling in the meter when you want heat or hot water. Jump out of bed; put in the shilling; jump back into bed until it was tolerable to get out and start your day. That was Aaron's task; no complaints. Aberdeen University was founded in 1495; a beautiful collection of granite buildings, an ancient cathedral, various residences, narrow cobbled streets and fine professorial houses. After a year, one of Aaron's professors generously invited us to live in their loft, and share their kitchen, in their historic granite house on The Chanonry in Old Aberdeen. Aaron was the key that opened that door. From there we explored Scotland in our second-hand Volvo – crossing the highlands purpled with heather, stopping in Bed 'n Breakfasts, visiting the Balmoral Highland Games hoping to shake hands with the Queen. What are those strange pointed things popping up everywhere above the heather? Who knew hares had such long ears? In Canada I only know bunnies with floppy ears. And climbing the north-facing corrie of Loch Na Garr memorialized by Lord Byron -

England! Thy beauties are tame and domestic,
To one who has roy'd on the mountains afar,
O for the crags that are wild and majestic,
The steep, frowning glories of dark Loch n Garr.

And passing the cairns marking the misstep of an unlucky climber. Both of us were studying hard in our different fields. It was also socializing at the ubiquitous British Council – meeting Nigerian and every other African student; discussing, arguing, critiquing and planning the development of different countries, honing leadership skills – all the while not appreciating the role of institutions such as the Council, designed to replicate the British model of progress. And there was racism, here too. Nasty notes slipped under the door. Interesting people who challenged us in Edinburgh included the widow of one of those brilliant-by-necessity Igbo scientists, blown up by his own bomb lobbed at attacking federal soldiers. She had recently escaped from Biafra and was picking up the pieces of her shattered life, with her unruly children. Of course, unruly. Death, starvation and bombs will do that. A strong woman. Could I be so strong? Her drafty, dull apartment was a meeting place – jollof rice, egusi and ogbono soup – for debates, discussions which were always hopeful. No war is a good war. We visited Stirling late at night with Sir Francis Ibiam's daughter – a close friend and fellow student at Aberdeen Infirmary – looking for the small manor house shared by five elderly spinsters who had dedicated their youth and beauty as missionaries in the Eastern Region, and together are the collective Godmothers of our friend. To wake them, we banged on the big brass bell which had formerly hung in a Methodist Church in Umuahia. We met future politicians and leaders – Prof. Jerry Gana was a fellow student; many years later in Cote d'Ivorie I met the Minister of Foreign Affairs there and we reminisced about out time together in Aberdeen. *The long, long silver threads.* I completed my midwifery and went on to trainings in neonatal intensive care and public health – while Aaron completed his MA and was accepted for his PhD. But we needed money with a baby on the way. We were finished with Aberdeen for the time being. It was too soon after the civil war to return to Nigeria, so said by our relatives. Where is the next circle?

We disembarked in Lusaka, Zambia on December 12th, 1971. I was pregnant, expecting our first child in late February. Following the packing out of the flat and lengthy flight, the blasting heat on arrival, and the dusty drive on an interminable bumpy road, we arrived at Chikankata in southern Zambia. Chikankata is a rural mission compound comprised of a secondary boarding school, a hospital and staff accommodation. All staff were white expatriates. Aaron was contracted as the vice-Principal, a nod to diversity, prompted by a friend in Canada as a stopping place on our way to Nigeria. Our three years in Chikankata gave us our two sons, the first born in January 1972, the second in June 1973. Our first son, born prematurely, was placed in a pale blue painted wooden box covered by glass and heated by a light bulb. Having just come from a neonatal intensive care unit, I was searching for an oxygen tank – and found it on the furthest side of the hospital in the OR. Even so, all was well, he thrived and made up for his early entrance, and welcomed his brother. They were given their Igbo names. I worked in the maternal and child health care clinic attached to the hospital catering for long lines of Zambian women. We went for family walks – one son on Aaron's shoulders, the other tied to my back - to the nearby villages; learning a few Tonga words, absorbing the enervating impact of settler colonialism on east African communities. So different from the dynamism, dignity and pride of West Africa. In this rural Zambian setting, as a couple we were a racial anomaly; we were stared at, pointed to, giggled at. It wasn't a problem. Far away from the guidance and/or interference of either of our families, we could only look to ourselves, and consolidated our relationship in the neutrality of this circle. By 1974 we were ready to shift once again.

From Chikankata we relocated to Mindolo Ecumenical Foundation, a pan-African centre in Kitwe, Zambia. MEF is an international ecumenical education institution supported by, among other agencies, the World Council of Churches, and during our time, various UN agencies.

Aaron was appointed Dean of Studies, and I worked outside MEF in the Kitwe School of Nursing as a public health tutor. In this circle we had stepped into the defining moment of both our lives. Up to that point we were good people, happy in our world, trying to live around the few anomalies. MEF presented us – right in our faces - social injustice, inequality, unfairness, and an alternative perspective – social action against injustice; the imperative to respond. This period marked the struggle for liberation in southern Africa: Rhodesia, Namibia, Mozambique, Angola and South Africa. Zambia was a Front Line State in this struggle, housing liberation movements (South Africa's ANC, Namibia's UNITA, and Zimbabwe's ZAPU, and ZANU) from contested countries. As such, Zambia was on the receiving end of bombings and violence with South African airplanes overflying Zambian airspace, and assassinations of freedom fighters in Lusaka and Kitwe. And MEF was actively engaged, under UNHCR auspices, providing a range of soft trainings – such as, leadership and communication skills, media and journalism, youth leadership and governance, early childhood teacher education, business management, and art and design - importantly where artistic expression is a signifier of what can't be spoken – all with a view to enabling the success of soon to be liberated countries. Art began to fill our walls. Also MEF trained youth from across Africa engaged in these same skills, I remember students from Nigeria, Malawi, Ethiopia, Kenya, and Sierra Leone, to name some. A heady time when I was often on my own keeping the home front. Aaron was frequently travelling in Europe, East and West Africa with respect to WCC, UN and liberation activities; he also returned to Aberdeen for six months to complete his PhD. We welcomed these youth into our home, learning about their lives, experiences, cultures, cuisines, challenges, dreams and hopes. For many, it was a break from remembering experiences I could not even imagine. One time, I was sitting around the dining room table with two young Namibians (UNITA combatants) when my pressure cooker exploded. I ran to the kitchen laughing at the beans now stuck to my kitchen ceiling. I found our guests sheltering under the table shielding themselves from the illusory bombs raining down on them. Different experiences, different responses. Our sons thrived attending the international nursery on the compound, and later the grade school in Kitwe. Did I really let my little children climb up into the back of an open truck along with twenty-or-so other children laughing and screaming, rain or shine, going to school in Kitwe? And one of those children, an age-mate of my sons, now lives in Toronto and visits me regularly. We visited friends in Malawi, the newly independent Zimbabwe, Tanzania, Kenya, and Uganda, and met some of them again in other circles. The *long silver threads* of life-long friends. We made two visits to Nigeria during that time – meeting the extended family for the first time in Umuahia and Jos – really good people. I was given my Nigerian name *Ezinwanyi* – a good woman. We were exploring possibilities for return.

But there was also my personal crisis. Going into the children's ward one morning with the Nigerian pediatrician – (in addition to being a Front Line State, Zambia also supported the Biafran side of the Nigerian civil war. Hence, there was an active Igbo community in Zambia) – he pointed out that this cot and that cot, and also that one and that one will be free for new children, as the current occupants will die of malnutrition before the end of the day! Kwashiorkor and starvation were endemic. What was I doing in primary health care audaciously teaching mothers how to feed their babies – when systemic issues, poverty and the conflicts in southern Africa was at root? That moment marked the end of my nursing career and the start of a new and ongoing personal, intellectual and professional journey encouraged and abetted by Aaron focusing on politics, policy and Nigeria.

In 1980 we departed Zambia for Toronto where I started an undergraduate degree in Political Science/African Studies, and Aaron was a Course Director at York University, a precarious employment that needed to be addressed. Aaron returned to Nigeria to actively prepare for our family settling there permanently. I fast-tracked my degree and the boys and I joined Aaron in Jos in 1982. Jos was an ideal location. Aaron's sister lived there, also friends from Aberdeen – *silver threads* - were at the University of Jos and Aaron had made friends through the 'UniJos hotel community' – comprised of newly appointed academic staff awaiting housing in Senior Staff Quarters. When the house was ready Aaron came to collect us and we arrived in Kano in the middle of *hadj*. Stepping off the plane in the evening the air was filled with smoke from the scores of small fires built around the airport by pilgrims awaiting their flights to Mecca. Surreal, dreamlike. In the morning stepping out of the hotel to begin the drive to Jos, I saw an image indelibly imprinted on my brain – as real today as when I first saw it. The scene: a large, slow-burning garbage dump, absurdly located beside the hotel, with smoke gently wafting along with the odors. Through the haze across that dump walked a slender, tall, proud, handsome man in a cavernous azure blue *agbada*. A peacock, sophisticated, refined, and carrying his history and culture upon his being. The call to prayers resounding. The contradictions and contestations of a complex, rich culture. My introduction to the new circle.

We settled in the Jos Senior Staff Quarters; I learned to live with the water and electricity outages, and to navigate the markets – my relatives had a stall selling *akara*. We settled the children into the staff school initially, then into Hillcrest, an international mission school with an American curriculum. A family member joined our household – I was happy to welcome a female into the male dominated family circle. We met the neighbours and developed friendships. Aaron dug a well and planted his garden – a consistent feature of each of our homes. I met a group of Nigerwives and a few Niger-husbands from across the world, everywhere that young Nigerians had wandered – heard tales of resilience, learned hard lessons, was deeply impressed, and was supported – *long silver threads lasting to this day.* We returned to the village at Christmas. We attended weddings and naming ceremonies, wearing beautiful Nigerian cloths. Designing my own styles with Nigerian fabrics and finding a trusted tailor. I was overwhelmed by the austere and astounding beauty of Plateau State, the geological fascination of Shere Hills, which we explored regularly, climbing the rocks, Gog and Magog, crossing and poising against the instellbergs – those isolated rocky outcrop that dot the hills and dominate the skyscape. We met and made friends with local Hausa traders appreciating a modest glimpse into Nigeria's rich heritage of brass and leather artifacts, cloth, and carvings – Aaron collected and filled our house with such fullness. I completed my MA in Political Science/International Development at the University of Jos. It was challenging, a steep and at times, uncomfortable learning curve; maneuvering through the staff strikes; and always the fact, in pre-internet days, of inadequate resources for the needs of eager scholars. But I highly respected my professors and maintained relationships with them long after. We felt at home.

Even so, money was a problem as I was unemployed. With our extended family we started a pig farm close to Shere Hills – heavy work but charming animals, and we added pork to our somewhat soya bean/tofu heavy diet - the latter supplied by a fellow Nigerwife as her money-earning project. I went back to the university of Jos and completed a Diploma in Education that subsequently enabled my employment as a Grade 4 teacher in Hillcrest School. My salary went directly into the boys' school fees. I am friends to date with the mother of one of my students, and I still communicate with him – now working in Morocco. *Long silver threads.* Of course, there were the coups, December 1983, overthrowing President Shehu Shagari, with Major General Buhari assuming as Head of State. In August 1985, Major General Babangida overthrew Buhari; and the attempted coups that followed in December 1985 and again in 1990. Life under the military – the militarization of civil society, the enforcement of environmental clean-up, the marching, parading, the devaluing of education, the corruption and repression. Impoverishment, hardship. Life was becoming increasingly difficult, scary, with resources **were** stretched to the limits. In 1992 I was awarded a scholarship to study at York University, Toronto to begin my PhD program in political studies/political economy with a focus on military rule in Nigeria. I arrived in Toronto with our sons; they were so excited and proud as they exited the plane in their new second-hand clothes from Katako Market. A year later Aaron joined us, when he took his sabbatical leave at the University of Toronto. Carrying all we are, and had become, with us, we stepped into another circle.

The next few years Aaron remained in Toronto while I was in and out of Nigeria, and across Africa –for my doctorate research in Nigeria, and after a year once my course work was completed, as required for my job as the Africa Program Officer with an international development agency responsible for projects in southern, east, and west Africa, including Nigeria. When visiting Nigeria, Ghana, Sierra Leone, Cote d'Ivorie or Cameroon I would stop over in Lagos, or Umuahia to meet with family, to keep our connection strong. My job took on more urgency in Nigeria in 1994 when General Sani Abacha, who had cancelled the interim civilian government, issued a decree that placed his government above the jurisdiction of the courts, effectively giving him absolute power. During the subsequent dark days, as part of the Nigerian expatriate community in Canada, both Aaron and I became deeply involved with, and active in, advocacy with respect to the democratic struggle in Nigeria. With the closure of the Canadian High Commission in Nigeria in 1995, following Canada's aye vote at the Commonwealth Heads of Government Meeting to suspend Nigeria from the Commonwealth, Canada designed an in-Nigeria mechanism to support the democratic struggle within Nigeria. This project was managed by my agency and by Cuso, a Canadian NGO that I re-engaged with, in yet another future circle. Canadians were denied visas to Nigeria, but given my experience in Nigeria and the fact of my 'permanent residence' stamp in my passport enabled my entry. After the year, 2000, this was changed to a naturalized Nigerian passport – I was tasked and privileged to manage this project in Nigeria and in Canada. This involved many more visits to Nigeria, meeting activists and heroes of that period – Wole Soyinka, Isola Williams – the list is long. We supported NGOs to deliver democratic and human rights interventions – Civil Liberties Organization, Radio Kudirat – among others. Accompanied by activists brought to Canada under the project – Kayode Fayemi, Ayo Obe, Bilkisu Yusuf, Fr. Matthew Kukah, and Nkoyo Toyo – to name a few, we met regularly with Foreign Affairs Canada to inform and shape (on the basis of the experience of front line activists), Canada's foreign policy vis-à-vis Nigeria. I was based in Jos for varying and extended periods. I kept my connections to my Nigerwives' friends recognizing the hardship of that repressive period – more so in comparison with the relative security of my own position. I could go in and out. Aaron kept the home front during this period. And he was proud of the work I was doing – however small it was. These were the greatest gifts to me. In 1999/2000 when Nigeria returned to civilian government and Canada returned to Nigeria, when my doctorate studies were completed and Aaron had become a dual citizen, when our sons were starting their own independent lives, and after Aaron had retired, it all came together again. We were challenged with another circle – Abuja and diplomatic life – an unexpected and completely new experience. Consulting with our family in Canada and Nigeria we were advised via Umuahia: *Hapu ihe e dere na moto banye moto* – an Igbo saying meaning 'leave what is written on the motor and enter the motor' - indicating that taking action is a priority over having details or previous knowledge. We returned to Nigeria.

The turn of the century marked a reversal of our previous roles: I was the primary income earner now; Aaron was the accompanying spouse. In 2000 I was employed by Foreign Affairs, Canada tasked with re-establishing, after Canada's lacuna, and managing the locally-staffed office of the Canadian International Development Agency based in Abuja. The High Commission had just been re-opened and the various departments were being set up including the department wherein my office was positioned. Aaron and I arrived in Abuja and I set to work, finding and furnishing our accommodation - we chose not to live on the Canadian compound – our feet were in two communities. I identified an office space off-site from the High Commission, purchased equipment, imported vehicles and other trappings, employed staff, established our presence with other embassies and donor agencies, and delivered on the government of Canada's development priorities – the challenge was enormous. Aaron, now retired, was of immense help to me – we were a team comprised of an official and unofficial member. Within six months, the office was operational with a cadre of ten professional and support staff. By the time of our departure from CIDA in 2013 the office had relocated to larger premises to accommodate an expanded staff of 19 and a core group of 27 consultants. I was able to draw on some of the *silver threads* established in our earlier circles in Nigeria, and to build new *silver threads* to meet the human and institutional resource needs of thematic professionals, NGOs, contacts, advisors, consultants, and relationships enabling me to deliver on my tasks.

The next thirteen years (2000 – 2013) were very busy and enormously interesting for both Aaron and for me. We gained a glimpse of, and put our toes into the world of diplomacy with its language, nuance, subtleties, contradictions, and pretensions. It was a world where I engaged with, and off times appreciated individuals in the political class – I related particularly with the Ministries of Environment, Health, and Women's Affairs in accordance with Canada's international development priorities. Representing CIDA within a cadre of international donor agencies, I participated in an infinite number of high-level meetings, was a member of various elite donor committees – HIV/AIDS, constitutional amendment, election oversite to name some; contributed to, and facilitated the design of CIDA-funded projects at the federal and state levels. Canada's focus was Bauchi and Cross River States – hence hundreds of visits were made to those states during this time. In particular – only because it became the focus of our final circle – visits to Cross River were note-worthy, and numerous because of discussions of a possible large-scale youth entrepreneurship project to be supported by the Canadian government in Calabar. Meeting with actors, stakeholders, NGOs, political leaders, and youth activists in these discussions was very energizing. New *silver threads* were being spun. People trying hard to make a better life for unemployed and unemployable youth. It was a huge problem. Driving to Cross River State, Aaron would join me and drop off at Umuahia to be collected on the return trip.

There were State Dinners that I attended in both Nigeria and in Canada - President Obasanjo and Canadian Prime Minister Jean Chrétien had a warm relationship. There were biannual working/consultation trips for me, joined by Aaron, to Canada, and also to other countries – Ethiopia, Ghana, Benin, Mali, Sierra Leone, Mozambique, and South Africa. Also, Egypt, Jordan and Turkey – walking through an Istanbul market we were greeted with calls of *Kofi Annan, Kofi Anna!* Aaron was pleased as we had been told that Turks are racist. I was thankful for my Nigerian ECOWAS passport. And for my Nigerwife status, as it smoothed the off times fraught passage through Nigerian immigration. *You are our wife; away you go. No need to check the bags.* Aaron joined me at times and we would often stay on for a few more days if possible, exploring Luxor, Alexandria, Amman, Cape Town, and Addis Ababa.

We entertained Canadian government visitors both officially and unofficially in our home, taking them to local artists and artisans promoting Nigeria's rich heritage as Aaron's reputation as an amateur/expert grew. Similarly, we spent time with friends and colleagues from the Canadian and other diplomatic communities. Stimulating, vexed political conversations always, and in the face of evident anomalies in the daily lives of Nigerians, we promoted and evidenced in our house the beauty, richness, complexity, and possibilities of Nigeria's cultural heritage. 'Evidencing' refers to Aaron's deepening passion during this period for supporting Nigerian artistry, both young and established artists, and commissioning and collecting metalwork, furniture, wood carvings, paintings and ceramics. Bruce Onobrakpeya, Asiru Olatunde, and Ishola Osogbo hung on our walls. And tourist reproductions of 9th Century Igbo Ukwu bronzes and 17th Century Benin bronzes were researched by Aaron, and valued for their representation of complex societies co-existing with great European empires. All found a place in our house. Aaron and I, through the Nigerian Field Society, went on two archeological digs unearthing Nok culture led by the University of Frankfurt, Germany and the National Commission for Museums and Monuments. Nok culture co-existed with Greek and Roman civilizations. Our sons also picked up their father's interest in Nigerian art and crafts. We visited markets looking for particular artifacts – tourist baskets, masks, beadwork, cloth, clothes – that they had requested we look out for.

Our children and grandchildren visited us one Christmas, and again for my 60th birthday – we were off to the village, keeping our family ties tighter; to Jos to catch up on the pig farm and climb Shere Hills again – now more conscious of security issues. We took a trip to Yankari Game Reserve in Bauchi to swim in the natural warm spring – *watch out for those thieving monkeys!* We went to Obudu Ranch in Cross River State to walk the hills, *take note of Fulani cattle life atop the tallest Sankwala Mountains, and peek over into Cameroon.* This was also a period of assisting the next generation of our Nigerian extended family – the nieces and nephews struggling in or to enter university, and various trainings and apprenticeships – building their lives in an uneasy and harsh world. There were family weddings, naming events, funerals – all the events that bookend our Igbo life. Aaron was now the eldest in his village.

There were also troublesome memories. On our drive to Obudu Ranch to celebrate Christmas with our sons, grandkids and members of our extended Canadian family - in a two-vehicle entourage - all vehicles travelling that road were held to a stop at a police check point as security agents swept the road ahead clearing it of robbers. When cleared, we went on our way. . In the middle of the night in Asokoro, Abuja the sounds of gunfire erupted. Our compound was secured, but a neighbour had been shot in a robbery attempt. This is also a side of Nigerian life. And, for me, I was threatened with kidnapping; a ransom was demanded. The High Commission security division took this seriously and responded with doubling the number of security guards at our house; with two personal security guards accompanying me everywhere, a new leaded vehicle with doors I could not open unassisted because of the weight, a newly assigned driver who was security trained. I had access to the personal mobile number of the Chief of Police, Abuja with instructions that he could be called any time, day or night. The ransom demand was the equivalent of CAN$500 – three-quarters of the US$ equivalent. As Rosen notes in <u>Bargaining for Reality</u>, *like a price uttered in a bazaar, the true value is determined by the outcome of the bargaining engendered.* Perhaps the market price for a Nigerwife is less than that of other expatriates. After two months of awkwardness and people tripping over each other, it was deemed the threat had passed, and all extra security measures were withdrawn. It might have been worse. And my potential kidnappers had learned some lessons to be applied to their next kidnapping endeavour.

In 2013 I also retired and we returned to Toronto – both grey-haired and a bit creaky – and thinking, is this the final circle? We settled in, filled our house with collected artifacts that stimulated memories, triggering the when, where and meaning of the objects. Family dinners; following the lives of the grandchildren; a new daughter-in-law; a new grandson. Even so, and yet again, Nigeria came calling – in the form of Cuso, the NGO I had worked for during the democratic struggle. Cuso had been awarded the youth entrepreneurship project funded by CIDA. Was I interested in managing that project from the Canadian side? Of course, I was. So once again, back and forth to Nigeria over the next four years, with Aaron, when longer periods of stay were required – we spent six months in Calabar one year – or on my own when the visits were only ten days or so. Always with the stopover in Umuahia. I took pleasure and satisfaction from this circle – I believe the project, from which with its closure in 2019 I finally, finally retired – improved the lives of some young women and men. In a sense it was the culmination of our years together working on social justice issues, and for me, on international development.

Aaron was ill and after fifty years together he passed away at home surrounded by his family in August 2018. During his illness we were supported by *silver threads of family and friends* built up over the years from the various Zambian and Nigerian circles. Visitors would come; there was always room for *silver threads*. With Aaron's passing the gap is a hollowness fashioned from memories. We loved each other.

Of course, there were bad times, hard times, mistakes made, problems not solved that endured and coloured the future. But I can't really remember the details of those times. I only remember the shining moments. I am consistently a Nigerwife – no matter the geographic space. Over time my relationship with Nigeria – my adopted country – marked me deeply and broadened me. *Mma nyanyi bu di ya* – an Igbo saying meaning 'a woman's beauty is her husband'. I am a beautiful Nigerwife.

A Rose by any Other Name

Kanchana Ugbabe

I am not a rose, nor is she. If she were a rose but not called as such, would she still smell as sweet whatever she was? She is called by my name -Kanchana- one of those quirky ways in which people become connected to you whether you planned it or not. My name was mine. It belonged to only me. Not a common name but one which was lovingly bestowed on me by my parents. I was fondly called 'Kanch' by my family, much loved, cherished, and even indulged as a child. I had never come across another me, in school or college or university. It made me feel distinguished and set apart. There were two or three of Priyas and Lalithas and Kamalas wherever a list of names appeared, but always only one of me, Kanchana.

Women's names are very significant in my husband's Idoma culture. Names that recall situations, names that commemorate occasions, names that spell comfort and encouragement after a tragedy, names that bestow a blessing. Ochanya, Egajanya, Emiene, Inyamuwa, Onyumoi…..The other tricky part about Idoma names is that the name has to start with a vowel sound. If it didn't, a vowel would be added to the consonant. My name spelt trouble from the start.

A three-syllable name was bound to be mispronounced once I left my home territory. They called me 'kun-Chaana'. The accent was placed on the second syllable most of the time. It didn't sound like me, but I responded all the same. I got tired of correcting people. The music in my name was lost. My name meant 'gold'. I was the golden girl, rare, treasured, lovely, not something you casually stumbled upon. But they made it sound pedestrian.

My husband who knew how to pronounce my name stopped calling me by name once we got to Nigeria. 'Are you there?' was my name. That was often his way of calling me. If I didn't respond, he would follow it up with 'I am talking to you' in a tone, slightly louder. He referred to me as 'En'Onche', ('Onche's Mum) when speaking to the extended family.' I came to be called universally, in Nigeria that is, as the mother of our first son, Onche. En'Onche or Mama Onche. I too referred to my husband as 'Dad' (the children's Dad) or as 'Ad'Onche', Onche's Father, when speaking of him to a third person. It was a combination of cultures, Indian and Nigerian, that robbed us of our first names. In India, wives wouldn't dream of calling their husbands by name. It sounded cheeky, lacking in respect. As for 'Darling' or 'Honey', that was out for both of us. It just wasn't us.

In the meantime, the Nigerian custom of naming children after a family member or friend came our way. There are hosts of Aako's in the family named after my husband. Very confusing when every family has an Aako. Tinker, tailor, soldier, sailor, richman, poorman, big, small, fat, lean etc. My name being strangely different was not exempt from this custom. A relative who was pregnant had planned on naming her child 'Aako' out of admiration for my husband. The baby turned out to be a girl and became a 'Kanchana' instead. A case of mistaken identity but it was expedient that it remained so. It was not the umbilical cord but a name that connected me to this child. The girl grew up in the home town, she was light complexioned, skinny as she grew older, moody, and hard to please. Her mother, a single Mum found it difficult to pander to her daughter's whims. So before long, my namesake, my rose by no other name but mine, arrived at my house, a seven-hour bus ride from the home town where her mother lived.

We are not peas in a pod. We are very different as persons, this seventeen-year-old and I. I love books. She reads when there is an exam around the corner and treats books with scant respect. I have always been a dreamer. She is practical. She sweeps the compound to perfection, stands at the kitchen sink till every teaspoon is polished, church music being piped into her ears. She has a lovely voice. I keep my singing to the bathroom. Her lunch bag bulges with rice and stew, cake, boiled eggs and anything else she can lay her hands on first thing in the morning. There was a time when she carelessly threw food, medication, and unwashed plates under her bed. She has been cured of that and has become responsible and well informed as a citizen of the world.

My name is everywhere now. They yell out my name when there is someone at the gate. They shout my name when a family member needs help. They call out my name to peel the potatoes, buy a loaf of bread from the corner store, wash the dishes, or feed the birds. My namesake grew lanky and tall as a schoolgirl before putting on flesh, false eye lashes, and artificial tresses that came down to her waist. Graduating from school to college, she acquired an attitude. I too call her by her name, my name. My mirror image. It is awkward but we have adjusted to each other. I have become fond of her. I don't respond when my name is called because it is Rose No.2 that is being beckoned. My husband calls her by my name which is her name as well. He now calls me 'Mum' at every instant. At 72, I am Mother, the matriarch, Mummy, and Mum. He and I have become parents to each other as our first names have been bartered, sold, appropriated, claimed and discarded.

Nigeria: East, West, North – A Fruitful Life

Astrid M Clarke

Born in Bolton, Lancashire, England in 1941 during the 2nd World War, I was the only child of my parents who had been married for five years before I was born. My father was called John Prescott but went by the name Jack, and my mother was Mary Anne Elizabeth nee Briggs. Her name was a very popular name at that time. Her mother was a Mary Anne Elizabeth too. My mother always said if she ever had a baby girl with dark black hair, she would name her Astrid after Queen Astrid of the Belgians, hence my name. Queen Astrid who was loved by so many people worldwide, had married King Leopold III. By birth she was Princess of Sweden. She was only a Queen for less than two years and died in a car accident in 1935 in Switzerland. My mother kept all the newspaper articles of her life and her terrible death.

My schooling was basic so I attended the local Girls' Secondary Modern. No thoughts then of going to university as very few women attended university in those days. So at the age of fourteen, I attended a commercial academy for one year and left school at fifteen to work as a junior in an office of Manufacturing Chemists. I was very happy there for six years and got to know the ins and outs of running an office which helped me in later years when I started my own business. I attended night classes at Bolton Technical College to improve my shorthand, typing, and English. I also learned how to use the comptometer which we had in the office and which no one knew how to use. At the age of twenty-one I decided to find a position in the city of Manchester at GUS as a Comp operator and worked with the very first IBM Computer.

My husband to be, William Robertson Clarke, (whose mother was Nigerian, and father Australian) meanwhile, arrived in Bolton from Nigeria in 1957 to study at Bolton Technical College. He was sent on a scholarship by the CMS (Church Missionary Society). He ended his studies at the Royal College of Advanced Technology which later became Salford University. We met at the Bolton Technical College dances. He was a good dancer and full of personality. All my friends loved him. We got on well together and at first Willie would join me and my friends wherever we socialised. We courted for four years and during this time he left Bolton Technical College for Blackburn Technical College because they specialised more in the Building Trade that he had decided to study. I travelled by bus from Bolton to Blackburn every Saturday. We went dancing at the Mecca dance hall there. We would be the first on the dance floor and the first to leave because I had to get a bus back to Bolton before 11 pm to catch the last bus home. It was the same when he left Blackburn to study in Salford. The same again, last bus home.

The friendship between Willie and me in the 1950s wasn't seen with favourable eyes by some people. I was just seventeen years old. My mother was told by a friend's mother: 'If it was my daughter .....' My parents, on the other hand were wonderful. Willie was welcomed into our home. I remember the first day he was to visit our house, we were all very excited and thought it would be nice to play Ludo. We often played Ludo in our home and sometimes Mum got annoyed with Dad when he'd say he needed a 1 or a 6 to knock her out and he'd get it. We had expected we would have to show Willie how to play Ludo as coming from Africa we were convinced he wouldn't know how to play the game. How wrong we were! Willie knew the game better than us and he was the one teaching us new tricks. My parents realized we were determined to marry when I said: 'If Willie lived in the desert, I'd go there!'

Our wedding took place in December 1962. It was the coldest winter we had ever experienced but we looked forward to August when we would spend thirteen days sailing to Nigeria. Indeed \my first trip to Willie's country was a good experience aboard Elder Dempster's M.V. Aureol. We enjoyed the hot Oxo soup every morning until we reached warmer climes, then ice cream every morning at 11 am. We made good friends on the ship and learning about their experiences helped prepare me for my new life in Nigeria. I particularly remember an English lady who had lived in Lagos for a long time with her Nigerian husband, a tailor, and whose daughter had been crowned Miss. Nigeria. Later in Lagos, we were invited to her daughter's wedding and many important personalities were there including the President's wife, Flora Azikiwe.

The ship docked at Apapa, Lagos and what a wonderful reception it was! The band was playing and people were cheering. Everyone seemed to be meeting friends and relatives they had not seen for years. There were also expatriates returning after their three months' leave. Willie's brother Robert and his sister Edna with her husband Alex were there to greet us. When we had collected our trunk and belongings we were driven to Oshodi, a town on the outskirts of Lagos near the airport. It was a little bit of a shock seeing a lot of ram shackled houses on the way and I hoped we would live in a better house.

Auntie Edna's bungalow was very nice and I was really welcomed there. They spoke to me about what to expect living in a different environment than the one I was used to. They said I would probably experience culture shock, but assured me that they were there to help. They also gave us £70 to help us settle down. We stayed comfortably with them for a few days because of floods on the road to our destination at CMS Blaize Memorial Trade Centre, Abeokuta, Western Region where we did all our main shopping in Kingsway Stores. We had been given a beautiful bungalow and also a car by the Church Missionary Society (CMS). The CMS Blaize Memorial Trade Centre (named after Richard Olamilege Blaize born into a family of emancipated slaves of Yoruba origin) had sent my husband to the UK for training in the building field. The Trade Centre trained students in carpentry and joinery. Many of the church pews in Lagos were handcrafted by Blaize students. They also made 'squash' (a fruit drink), from the many fruits they grew on the compound. The squash became very popular in the big supermarkets. Their Guava Jelly was a speciality and was sold in a tin. We loved our stay there and I enjoyed playing the organ for their choir, teaching them the hymn 'I Vow to Thee My Country'.

We made many friends in Abeokuta but after eight months we were asked by the Bishop of Owerri to take up an appointment in Osusu, Aba, in the Eastern Region. Before this we had flown there for an interview. The Bishop, along with the World Council of Churches planned to take over a Grade III Teachers Training College and wanted my husband to help turn it into a Trade Centre. It was a very happy time in Aba and very rewarding for my husband. He started the Delta Trade Centre with just twelve students who helped in the construction of many of the school buildings and expanded to three hundred students. However, when we first arrived, I was quite upset with the accommodation. We had left a beautiful bungalow in Abeokuta for a new bungalow which was a poor substitute with no indoor toilet, many doors leading to the outside, and no electricity. The Bishop had bought us a kerosene fridge and what they called 'hard furniture' and an 'iron bed' with a mosquito net. Of course there were no glass windows, but wooden shutters. My husband said "Don't worry. I'll make it fine" and soon he converted it into a beautiful bungalow which many of our English friends thought lovely and cosy. It took some time to get electricity but when we did just before my father visited, we thought we were in heaven!

Aba was a good place to live then. There was a Club with an eighteen-hole golf course. We enjoyed Scottish Country Dancing every Saturday night where £1 each in the kitty would cover all the drinks for the night. We even had a pantomime. I participated in it and we performed at the Shell Club, in Port Harcourt one night.

Our son Simon Kayode, was born in August 1964, a month after my mother died in Bolton. He was born at the Queen Elizabeth Hospital, Umuahia, almost 40 miles from Aba. It was very dangerous to drive at night to Umuahia, as villagers along the route blocked the roads on account of armed robbers. This made us very anxious in case the baby arrived at night. However, the due date was delayed and I was already in hospital when the baby arrived.

I worked in Aba, first for the West African Drug Company in the mornings and for Chesebrough Ponds in the afternoons. I couldn't work full time anywhere because I had a British passport and could not be on a Company's expatriate quota. Not until I had agreed to give up my British passport and be given Nigerian citizenship could I get a full time job. This was how I was able to work as Secretary to the Managing Director, and the General Manager at Aba Textile Mills, an American company. I had filled all the forms for my Nigerian citizenship but it turned out to be just a matter of relinquishing my British passport. There was no provision for dual nationality then.

In 1967 the Eastern Region where we lived seceded from Nigeria and declared itself the Republic of Biafra. This led to a civil war and it became dangerous for us to remain in Aba, so we decided I should go to Lagos right away and Willie would follow. . I signed up for one of the British evacuation flights to Lagos from Port Harcourt. After waiting two days at the Presidential Hotel in Port Harcourt we were among the British women and children who were air lifted to Lagos. Prince William of Gloucester met us at Lagos Airport. He was working at the British High Commission in Lagos. (He was later killed in a crash in the plane he was piloting.). I was lucky to be also met in Lagos by the Manager of Aba Textile Mills Company Manager and I was taken to my sister-in-law, Edna's house in Oshodi. We were safe but worried about Willie who we had left behind.

As days passed, we began to get worried in Lagos as there was no sign of my husband and no phone to communicate with anyone concerning his whereabouts. Then suddenly, I don't know how many weeks later, he turned up in Oshodi, Lagos with security men. They hadn't believed what he told them about who he was, but after seeing the whole family welcoming him, they left him alone.

Willy told us how he had just managed to leave Port Harcourt on the last British ship into Lagos. He had planned to drive to Lagos in our car with some of our household items and he had paid someone to get him and the car across the River Niger. But it turned out that because of the military operations, the bridge had made impassable. Of course here was no boat and the money was lost. So he drove to Port Harcourt leaving everything he had packed in the car and gave the car to the SCOA Manager in Port Harcourt who gave him a cheque in French francs for the car. Willie told us how he had tied £100 under his foot as only £5 was legally allowed to be taken out, and boarded the ship. He had no passport. I had carried it with me because he had been born in Jos which was in Northern Nigeria and at that time the hostilities had put the lives of people from the North living in the East at risk. So, my husband had used my father's address in the UK on the travel documents. This was a terrible time.

We began to settle down in Lagos. I was able to continue working for Aba Textile Mills on the Lagos Marina and my husband got a lecturing position at Yaba College of Technology in the Civil Engineering Department. Unfortunately, he couldn't take up this position until September when the College resumed after their holidays.

My worst experience in Lagos came soon after Willie's arrival. I received a phone call in my office from someone at the General Post Office, just a few blocks from where I was working, with the terrible news that my husband had been arrested. They told me he was being kept at the Post Office and I must come immediately to identify him. I rushed there and found soldiers holding him, saying he was a mercenary. Of course, my husband had no ID as he hadn't started work. The soldiers took no notice of me and their English was not good so I rushed to call the highly respected Anglican Bishop of Lagos who had brought my husband up when he was young. Unfortunately when the Bishop arrived the soldiers didn't recognise him and didn't respect him as a Bishop. Seeing the cross and chains he was wearing they assumed he was a priest of the Cherubim and Seraphim religious sect. Worse still, the Bishop unfortunately mentioned that we had recently arrived from Biafra. On hearing this they sent for a vehicle to take my husband to Dodan Barracks the Military Head Office in Ikoyi. I tried to enter the vehicle as well and I was pushed off. So I headed to Dodan Barracks with the help of two Dutch employees from my office. We stood at the gates of the Barracks and could see my husband being paraded around outside their building under armed guard. I was hysterical and we rushed back to the office to phone the Bishop who was frantically trying to get in touch with some high-ups. A few hours later my husband unexpectedly walked into my office a free man. I could hardly believe it as most people arrested never came out of Dodan Barracks again. I was ill after that for some time. It shook me badly.

There were many incidents in Lagos during the Civil War. Biafran radio was sending out a lot of propaganda that all expatriates had left Lagos as the Biafran Army had reached Lagos. Although that was untrue, at one point in the early months of the war the Biafran army advanced across the River Niger and got as far as Ore in the Western

Region. That day was another terrible day. The traffic was unbelievable in Lagos. My husband was on his way with our young son in the car to pick me up, but little did I know that. When the traffic was at a standstill on the Marina, I decided to start walking home to Surulere. At the Carter Bridge, (then the only bridge linking Lagos Island to the mainland), I had to put my hands up and walk across the bridge. I walked as far as Ijora Causeway and luckily got a lift to Surulere. Reaching home, I found that no one was there. By the time my husband arrived back from Lagos Island it was after 10 pm and he was so annoyed with me for not waiting for him. (A mobile phone then would have been a blessing.) Luckily the Biafran military retreated and Lagos was never under threat of invasion. The traffic crisis had been caused by police checking all the vehicles entering Lagos.

Another time we had to rush out of Leventis Stores on the Marina as where a few of us used to congregate for lunch. There was heavy gunfire and a Biafran plane piloted by mercenaries was being shot at. Another time we ended up jumping out of the car into a ditch when we heard gun fire from the naval base on Ijora Causeway.

In January 1970 Biafra surrendered and the civil war ended. Despite this, there was rarely a time when Nigeria was crisis free as successive governments were overthrown. But life went on.

I laugh today when remember how I used to travel by bus from Yaba to Tinubu Square for work in and the passengers used to scramble through the windows. On one occasion when I was returning home from work I was number one in the queue for the bus, but I was not able to get on it because of the people pushing and forcing there way. Ordinarily I would wait for the next bus, but one day I got fed up doing that so I pushed my way onto the bus just like everyone else. I was cursed by a man on the bus all the way home!

From Surulere we moved to Yaba to be closer to the College where Willie worked. At this time I had gone back to UK as my father was ill. My father died in May 1970 and I returned to Lagos soon after. The house in Yaba we had moved into was a very colonial bungalow with wooden floors, on stilts. It was situated on the Yaba College of Technology compound. We used to go very early in the morning to buy our meat at the market before the flies got to it. The Yoruba markets in Lagos were different from the Aba market where we had done all our shopping. The Igbo traders seemed to be more efficient to me and if they didn't have what I wanted, they would go and find it for me. This was not the case in Yaba market where it was mostly women selling goods. Shopping there one day, they started abusing me for no reason until my husband rebuked them in Yoruba. They had a shock that he knew their language. Only then did they apologise to us.

After working for Aba Textile Mills I had to leave because the Mill closed down. I joined Transcap Travel Agency, part of the CFAO French company. I learned all about the travel business from them. I moved to Ikeja to open an office there for them. It was convenient for me as Simon had started to attend Grange School, Ikeja.

However by this time the number of cars on the roads in all parts of Lagos had far exceeded the available road networks. Consequently what would be a twenty minute journey normally, would take three hours on an average day. Lagos authorities tried to solve the problem by introducing alternating 'even number' days and 'odd number' days according to the last digit on the number plate of the car. We were only allowed to drive in designated parts of Lagos on alternating days depending on whether we were an even or odd car. Unfortunately this didn't have a lasting effect and Lagos traffic continued to be characterised by "go slow". It got so bad that after picking Simon from school we often did not reach home before 9pm. It was because of this that we decided to send Simon to school in England when he turned 8 years of age.

After ten years at the Transcap Travel Agency, Ikeja, I opened my own travel business. I also opened an office in Victoria Island, Lagos. By this time, expatriate women married to Nigerians were permitted to work but we had to have our husband's consent to do so. A special permit had to be stamped and signed by my husband.

After nineteen years in Lagos, in 1986 we decided to move to Jos in Northern Nigeria in and engage in farming. Our son would join us as he had completed his course at the Royal Agriculture College in England and was married. Jos was very different from Lagos. It had lovely temperate weather being 4,000 ft. above sea level and was very picturesque with mountains, and roses growing all the year round. We also acquired a wonderful addition to our family. Amina, the daughter of my husband's brother brought joy to our home and is still bringing me joy until this day. We built a lovely house on our farm in Barkin Ladi, about 30 miles from Jos. Our son and my husband ran the farm.

I opened another Travel Agency in Jos.

We had some very famous people arrive in Jos for the filming of 'Mister Johnson' (the book written by Joyce Cary) in the late 1980s. Also, Simon did the shooting in the film for Edward Woodward. Pierce Brosnan took the main lead as the DO (District Officer). I have a nice photo taken with Pierce Brosnan. Life in Jos was peaceful and slow-moving compared to Lagos and Aba. There were many expatriates in the town, an American school, cultural activities that kept us socially engaged. Living in a beautiful home on the edge of the farm had its own charm too.

Unfortunately in 2001 a tragic conflict between the Christians and Muslims Jos broke out. There was discord and turmoil that we had not experienced before. Jos was no longer the same Jos as when we arrived. It was so painful to see. I think 2001 was the worst in terms of ethnic and religious riots. We had everyone's cows on our farm for safety. Also, we had the Christian villagers from Zat and Barkin Ladi stay at our home every night for a few weeks because of rumours that terrorists from Mali were out to attack them. The village of Barkin Ladi had been barricaded so no strangers could enter. Local Muslims and Christians did their very best to keep the trouble makers out. I was still running my travel agency in Jos. In the midst of the conflict my son and I had to get to our office in Jos from Barkin Ladi to arrange for a group of women travelling to the United States for a conference. Although the road was closed, Simon decided to try to get through. We reached the blockade just before Jos Airport and the men there with their faces painted white saw our son and immediately allowed us through the blockade. It appeared they knew Simon because he used to teach them to play rugby. We got to Jos after passing through many hurdles. Along the way we saw mosques that had been set on fire. Many men had been killed and we saw bodies strewn on the road along the way. It was a terrible sight. Women and children were being rounded up and taken to the airport for safety. We finally got to my office and I quickly arranged for the group of women to pick up the British Airways tickets in Abuja. On arrival home we heard the terrible news of the 9/11 tragedy in New York. Of course, the group could not attend their conference again. All flights were suspended.

From 2001 onwards, Plateau State, where Jos is located, was wracked by intermittent ethnic and religious violence. In March, 2004, Willie and I retired and moved to Conwy. N. Wales. But sadly my husband died in the UK just six weeks after retiring. Even in the years after we had left Nigeria and Simon was running the farm there was no real peace. Farms were often attacked by Fulani herdsmen. On one occasion bullets were shot through the windows of our house in Barkin Ladi. After leaving our farm, the Fulani herdsmen went over the river to a village and killed many people. That evening Simon sent me messages on my mobile phone. Luckily my son was safe but they were troubling times.

Simon continued to live in Jos but sadly died of meningitis on 15th January 2018. It is heart breaking as our son loved Nigeria and chose to remain there. I'm consoled by the fact that he is buried in St. Pirans churchyard in Jos, with his grandfather, an Australian, who died of yellow fever in 1938 in Jos.

Willie's father fought in WWI in the 1st Division Engineering Corp, Australian Imperial Forces He arrived in Jos, Nigeria in the early 1920s. He lived in Bukuru, Jos, and after his death his house was turned into the famous Yelwa Club for the ATMN (Amalgamation of Tin Miners. Nigeria). He was a miner engaged in tin-mining all over the Barkin Ladi area, even where our farm later came to be situated. We named the farm after him 'Dan Maikatako Farms' meaning the 'man who is like a plank of wood, unbending'. He was well liked by the Nigerian tin miners. My husband's father was also a Major in the West African Frontier Forces. St. Pirans Church in Jos was built by these tin miners.

My husband's mother, Hadiza lived in the village of Jong, Barkin Ladi. Her father worked as a driver for the Tin mining company called Keffi Tin. She was brought up a Muslim, spoke Hausa and could not speak English. She travelled to Lagos to greet us when I first arrived in Nigeria with my husband. Later, when we moved to Jos, we lived close to where she lived. She was a hardworking and pleasant person. She died in September, 2001. We never did know her true age as births were not registered in those days. However, I am sure she was well into her 80s.

Our life in Nigeria had its ups and downs. I never thought of leaving Nigeria even after the airlift from Biafra. I wanted to stay by my husband's side as I had married for love. I enjoyed working in Nigeria and had a lot of good employees, although I did have my fair share of frauds in my offices. I was always accepted in society and respected. My husband's family was very accommodating and I am still in contact with all my nieces and nephews there. The older relatives have passed away. Amina, now our daughter, attended Hillcrest School in Jos until she was twelve years of age. She completed her education in Britain, and having studied law, she was called to the Bar at the Inner Temple in 2006.

I gradually acquired a taste for Nigerian food but at the beginning it was a bit strange .I loved Jollof rice and pepper chicken. I didn't have problems with the language as most people spoke English. A sense of humour and compassion brought me through all those years I spent in Nigeria. Looking back over my forty-one years in Nigeria, my eyes were opened wide. As an only child, a little spoilt, I learnt a lot about life over the years. I have no regrets. Taking the rough with the smooth, making do with what you have and what God has given you makes one a better person. A great experience! Thank you, Nigeria!

Well Done!
Joanne Umolu

When we lived on the construction site of Kainji Dam in what is now Niger State in the mid-1960s my favourite way to travel south to Lagos or Ibadan was to go by train. The old narrow gage passenger trains were a popular means of transport then and I thoroughly enjoyed riding on them. Once when I was escorting my mother to Lagos, we reserved one of the private first class compartments. It had two comfortable seats on either side of a big window that we could open wide or a folding table below the window that we could pull open. A bunk was attached to one wall to lie on if we needed to sleep during the long journey. The first class compartments were serviced by a porter who brought us tea and hot meals. Less comfortable, but more interesting to me, were the coaches with rows of seats like on a bus. There I joined many other passengers and tried my best to find a window seat. The coaches were always lively, voices of chatter and sometimes arguments were accompanied by the shake and rattle of the train. Tired mothers would be surrounded by an assortment of bags, boxes and even a pot of cold rice or yam with which they attempted to sooth their restless children. Amazingly, there were always some people who slept soundly through it all.

Inevitably beggars would also be on a train going south. At any station in the North there would be a gathering of disabled men, and sometimes women, of all ages. Some had become crippled from polio , the limbs of others were deformed from leprosy and other were blind. The blind beggars were always accompanied by a lean and shabby young boy or girl who cared for them on the train and led them when they started begging on the streets. The beggars waited beside the train while it was stopped and just as the train started to pull out they would dash for the steps and enter the train. Perched on a space on the floor they embarked on a free, but difficult, journey to the big city of Lagos where they anticipated making more money begging than in the North.

The journeys were very long, the trains moved slowly but not smoothly. (I once tried to drink a cup of tea while the train was moving – not possible.) I especially enjoyed the frequent stops in towns along the way to allow passenger to get off and on. Looking through the window, the scene was always colourful. New passengers laden with luggage struggled to reach the door to our coach in time to get a good seat. .There was continuous movement on the crowded platform where families gathered to welcome a new arrival, loads of all shapes and sizes were pushed on trolleys, and beggars who thrust their tin bowls expectantly toward any well-dressed person in the crowd.

I was especially fascinated by the "market" that took place through the open windows of the train. Immediately the train came to a stop women and young children who had been waiting at the station rushed to the train windows with bread, bottles of drinking water and soft drinks and local fruits and vegetables. . I enjoyed watching the lively transactions taking place at every window, accompanied by the laughter and arguing that were part of the bargaining going on in Pidgin English and local languages. Especially in the south there were plenty of oranges and bananas, pineapples, and papaya for the passengers to buy as well as roasted maize if it was in season. Further north, groundnuts, bean cakes and bottles of *kunu*, a refreshing maize based drink, were favourites for the passengers. I too made some purchases, although, as an obvious expatriate I inevitably paid the *oyinbo* price despite my desperate attempts to bargain. During one stop in a Yoruba town I bought a thorn carving of a palm wine tapper from a little boy who told me he had carved it himself; I liked it so much I didn't even attempt to bargain.

I remember once when I was sitting in a coach going north I was as fascinated as I watched a woman sitting near me. She must have sent messages to her friends and relations in the towns we would pass through, since on several of our stops going north groups of people rushed to her window for a brief but joyous reunion. While we were in the south where fruits were abundant I had been surprised to see her buy so many pineapples, coconuts, oranges and bananas that they filled up the seats next to her. Hours later when we stopped at towns further north where fruits were not grown locally it was heartwarming to watch her as she would quickly pick up some of the fruit she had bought in the south and pass it back out the window to the groups of relations and friends who had come to greet her.

It was always dark by the time I disembarked, exhausted from the long journey but still savoring the memories of experiencing Nigeria by rail. .

In 1966 we relocated to Port Harcourt. Unlike the construction camp we lived in at Kainji Dam, Port Harcourt was a busy city and a road leading to the centre of the town went right in front of our house. Very early on weekday mornings the first sounds we would hear from the road would be the footsteps of many people walking briskly down the road on their way to work. Jovial greetings would emerge from the steady stream of people passing by. Gradually, maybe an hour later, the sound of footsteps would be replaced by the sound of bicycle bells. Now the road would be filled with black Raleigh bicycles ridden by those workers who were fortunate enough to have a means of transport that allowed them to leave for work a little later. The cyclists accompanied their cheerful greetings with vigorous ringing of their bicycle bells. Gradually the number of cyclists would reduce and the road would become quiet. Finally it was the turn for the cars to take over the road. Unlike the first wave of pedestrians and the second wave of cyclist, the cars came one by one, as the senior management staff, then mostly expatriates, enjoyed a leisurely and quiet drive to work.

When we lived in Lagos in the 1970s we often made road trips around Nigeria. In those years there was only one place where a traveler could confidently expect to find a comfortable place to sleep and have a meal. And that was in the Cantering Rest Houses that the government established to meet the needs of civil servants on tour. My memories of the Catering Rest Houses my family stayed in when we travelled are of slightly shabby colonial style structures set in the midst of flowering shrubs and ancient trees. Each room opened up to the outside. So in the evenings, if we needed to escape the heat being redistributed in the room by a noisy ceiling fan, we could sit outside on the steps to our room. There we would relax from our day's journey and catch the cool evening breeze accompanied by the sound of crickets and the aroma of smoke from distant wood fires.

Food was served in the Rest House restaurant. The menu was limited but we could always count on a good meal of rice and stew or egusi or okra soup and *eba* when we arrived in the evening. In the mornings we would resume our journey after a hearty breakfast of eggs and porridge. There was one exception however. Once when we took our breakfast in Lokoja I swear I was served a second hand omelet. It looked suspiciously like the one I had seen on a plate someone at the next table had returned untouched a few minutes earlier. I can't remember if I ate it or not, but up to today I associate Lokoja with second-hand omelets.

Whenever my mother visited us she was always enthusiastic about the road trips my husband took us on There was one day we were driving somewhere in the Southwest when we were a long way from any town where we there would be a restroom to use. So when my mother and I felt the need to ease ourselves my husband pulled off the road near where there was some fairly thick bush. My mother and I walked away toward the bush while my husband stood beside the car to wait for us. A farmer came along and asked my husband if there was a problem. My husband explained that he was waiting for his wife and mother-in-law who had needed to visit the bush. So the friendly farmer stayed and chatted with my husband while he waited for us. Before long mother and I confidently left the bush and headed to car, certain that we had accomplished everything without having been seen. To our shock we discovered that a strange man was standing by our car with my husband. When we reached them the man smiled and greeted us with a cheerful "Well done!" We kept silent. We had no idea how to respond to that greeting. But when we drove off we all burst out laughing.

Life in Gwoza

Kathleen Gula

I was born in Newcastle upon Tyne, England 27th July 1940. I was a war baby and Newcastle was being badly bombed so my mother took me to a small village in the Lake District. My maternal grandmother was working there as an assistant nurse. My maternal grandfather had died during the Spanish flu of 1920. My paternal grandfather was a blacksmith and was one of the ones who made the bouncing bombs (All very secret).

My father was a soldier in WW2 in India. I remember he brought my sister, Jean, who was 2 and a half years younger than me, lovely bags made from skins. But whenever we went on walks the dogs would follow us!! I remember starting school in a one room classroom with only a few pupils in each year. It was great fun.

Later we moved back to Newcastle and I continued Primary School. This was the school my father had been to as a boy. We got a lot of snow in the N.E. of England We were living at the top of a hill and used to enjoy sledging down this hill when it snowed. Secondary

School was next and when my father's job took him to N. Ireland I continued Secondary School there. Nursing and Midwifery training followed in England.

It was while I was studying nursing in England that I first heard of a place called Gwoza in Nigeria. In 1960 a missionary couple came to speak about their work in Gwoza, a town in Northern Nigeria in what was then called Sardauna Province. I was so inspired by listening to them I knew Gwoza was where I wanted to work as a nurse, so I immediately began to prepare for mission work there. Little did I know that Gwoza would be my home for nearly 60 years or that was where my future husband lived.

Finally, after 3 years of preparation, in October 1963, I said goodbye to my parents and brother and sister who accompanied me to Liverpool where I boarded a boat bound for Nigeria. Saying goodbye was a bit emotional. Would I ever see them again in this life? But I was very excited that at last I was going to Nigeria. It was very rough in the Bay of Biscay but it was lovely and calm for the rest of the three week journey to Lagos.

Lagos--it was so hot!! From Lagos I was taken for orientation by my Mission to Panyam, a village near Jos, present capital of Plateau State in Central Nigeria. At last, on 10th Dec. 1963 I was taken to Gwoza over 500 miles from Jos. When I reached there I had the feeling that I had come home. And I loved every minute of the first 6 years I spent there.

"Maraba da zuwa", Welcome. These were the first words I heard in Hausa when the nurses came out to greet me on arrival at Gwoza in the N.E. of Nigeria, 10th December 1963. "Oh, Dr Chandler, (the pioneer missionary doctor to Gwoza in 1956) has brought his second wife." "Oh no." said Dr Chandler immediately, "She is my daughter." From that day on folks thought of me as an addition to his three children who were then in the UK, but had earlier lived in Gwoza.

Life was busy working on the wards in the in the Gwoza Hospital. We had main wards but also some round huts for some of the patients which I was in charge of. I was surprised to sometimes find the patient lying under the bed and a relative on the bed. *"Did this white sister not know that one respects the older person looking after the sick person"!!*

I learned to climb the Gwoza Mountains to pay regular visits to the mountain villages with some of the Nigerians. I had never climbed a mountain in UK but I was soon able to climb up and down only getting dizzy now and again during our decent. We took medical supplies to the mountain villagers, preached to them and did literacy work using reading cards. *"How silly of the white person to think that a reading card was not to eat!"*

Anyway, we soon showed them the use of the cards and many learnt to read and help each other.

Many of the villagers had never seen a white person who was friendly and wanted to help, unlike the British District Officers who usually visited them to collect taxes. Soon the adults accepted me and when they saw us coming would run down the mountains to carry our bags. The women always amazed me, many highly pregnant, carrying a baby on their back tied with a skin, and also carrying a sack of grain on their heads and climbing the mountains. This was a different culture and I knew no English person would be able to do that. At first the children hid from me but a ball works magic and soon they would be coming out of hiding and touching my white skin. Eating their food, even when covered with flies, soon cemented our friendships. When on the mountains I had the privilege of seeing some of the traditions of these people. Some of them were rather distressing. Once I watched a death ceremony. The women and men danced and wailed while beating themselves with thorns. They would throw themselves onto thorn fences. They would stop dancing as soon as the music stopped and then resume when the music restarted. This would go on for days. Another time I watched a witchdoctor treat a sick person. He slaughtered a sheep and smeared the dung of the animal on the sick person.

We as UK missionaries were always respected by Christians, Moslems and Traditional Religious worshippers. We enjoyed fellowship with many and were always invited to any special Moslem celebrations.

There were eight local languages but the one that united us was Hausa so that was the language I had to learn. As I was learning Hausa I often made mistakes; but fortunately I could laugh with the patients who corrected me. I also tried to learn some of the greetings in the other languages but we always had a nurse with us who knew many of these languages and could translate.

I was able to keep my family in UK informed of my work in Gwoza by sending them slides. They developed a keen interest in Gwoza and used to show my slides in various churches. Thus my home community became interested in the work I was doing. The young people used to knit vests and roll bandages from old sheets or pieces received from a factory for the Gwoza Hospital which my parents would send us in big containers. It was especially exciting at Christmas to receive a parcel my parents had posted in September which always contained a Christmas cake, pudding and many other treats.

In 1966 I returned to UK and enjoyed six months with my family and friends. In September of 1966 I returned to Nigeria and flew into Kano, the major airport in Northern Nigeria, only to land in the midst of a serious crisis. There had been a series of coups in Nigeria that year which resulted in serious political tensions between the Muslim North and the Christian South. This had led to hostility among the Muslims against Southerners who lived and worked in Northern Nigeria, especially against the Igbos of South East Nigeria. I arrived in Kano just when the hostilities had erupted again into widespread attacks on Igbos throughout the North including Kano. There was tension at the Kano airport which was filled with expatriates trying to flee the violence, so I stayed close to them. We were taken to a hotel to wait for a plane that was expected to fly to Lagos with a stopover in Jos where I was to report to our Mission Headquarters. To our dismay, those of us who were going to Jos had been forgotten about and we were left in the hotel. We were relieved when someone phoned the airport from our hotel and a bus was sent to take us to meet our plane at the airport. My heart sank when just as we reached the airport we saw our plane taxing down the runway. We all yelled and one of the airport officials ran up the tower to alert the pilot. Thankfully, the plane came back, we got into the cockpit where the pilot was and then moved into the main part of the smallish plane and flew to Jos. It had become dark when we reached Jos and there were no proper landing lights at the airport, but the pilot landed safely, dropped me and others off and went on to Lagos. But when I arrived, I discovered there was no one to meet me and that there was a curfew. Thankfully an airport attendant kindly drove me to our Jos Mission Headquarters. Greatly relieved, I opened the door of the Mission Office, only to be greeted with "Why have you come?" They then told me a telegram had been sent to our Mission in London telling me not to come, but the telegram never arrived. The next day some of us were out dressing the wounds of Igbo victims of the attacks. This was a lovely start to a second tour!!

After I returned from my leave I continued working in the Gwoza Hospital. It was during this time I met Daniel Gula who was working in one of the villages, nine miles from Gwoza, as a Pastor. Although our backgrounds were very different we shared similar values and interests as we were both committed to our work with the Gwoza people. Despite some skepticism and even opposition, we decided to marry. Our wedding took place on 30th October 1971 in the Gwoza Hospital Church. Many Moslems from the town came to the church to attend our wedding. In fact the Church was so full of our Moslem friends that some of the Christians had to stand outside! Those that had earlier opposed our marriage eventually came and apologized as they realised we were happy and complimented each other in our Church work.

Our first home for a few days was one of the small round huts on the hospital compound. The Church then moved us to Guduf Kasa, a small village near Gwoza town, where we lived in a small mud house. The house was small but we did not have much furniture, only a bed and mattress, a trunk that we put some cushions on, a small table and a few chairs. There were no mod cons or electricity. But this was our life and we were happy. We enjoyed sitting outside under a thatched veranda at night under the stars. All was not always peaceful, however. One night, as we were enjoying sitting outside, a flying snake passed over us. Another time a small snake came into the house and I jumped onto a chair (very brave!!) The cat soon got rid of it.

We always had some young people living with us. There were a couple of rooms in the compound so they lived there. They helped in the house especially the cooking as I knew I would not be able to cope with cooking on a wood stove and also with drawing water from the nearby well. I have weak arms and found I hadn't the strength to do heavy work. Moslem friends would ask Daniel, 'Does your white wife eat our type of food?" "Yes" he would answer, "and she can cook it too."

We were very happy. We had each other and we helped each other with different aspects of the work we were involved in. Daniel and I visited villages together preaching, teaching reading and doing medical work. We had one bicycle. Daniel would pedal and I would sit on the carrier and off we would go. We especially enjoyed how the people would wave at us as we rode past them.

In the early days of our marriage if we wanted to go to Maiduguri, 100 miles away, there were no buses so we had to use big lorries. Getting up into the back of the lorry was always a problem. Daniel had to help me up (or should I say, push me up) into the back of the lorry where we would sit on hard benches among many other passenger. I remember one journey when we suddenly hit a big pothole. "Oh dear" I exclaimed as I found myself on the lap of the man behind!! For the rest of the journey Daniel held on to me.

Daniel would keep me right about customs. Receive things with two hands and always give with the right hand. Curtsey when greeting and don't shake hands unless the person offered you his hand. There were surprises too. On our first Christmas I put a lot of *chin chin* (local biscuits) and sweets on a plate for our visitors, thinking they would eat a few and leave the rest for the next visitors. But as they left all the *chin chin* and sweets went into their pockets!! Never leave a tea bag in the cup as one of our friends decided to eat the bag!!

Daniel was always good at visiting Christians, Moslems and Traditional Religious people. I would sometimes go with him and we were always well accepted. When UK visitors or people from the Plateau visited us we always took them to visit the Chief and he insisted we sat on seats and not on the floor which was the custom of the Chief's Palace.

For the birth of our first child, Ruth October 1972, we had amazing help from one of our Moslem friends. He offered to help if we ever needed it. Just a few hours later I went into labour and as the hospital was 20 miles away Daniel didn't want to take me on the bicycle. So he went to our friend and he took me on the back of his motor cycle on very rough roads in the middle of the night. Not long after arriving I delivered and I always jokingly told people, "Ride on rough roads on a motor cycle and you will deliver quickly"!! Sadly, Ruth lived for only three months. The loss was painful, but this experience helped me to sympathise with those who lost children as so many had in our area.

When the next baby was due in 1974 we were offered a place in a small plane to take us to Jos from Maiduguri. This was Daniel's first ride in a plane and he was sitting in the front with the pilot and I was behind. When the Pilot went into auto-pilot and began reading his book Daniel's face would have made a good picture!! We reached Jos safely and our daughter Eli was born 27th June 1974.

Back in Guduf Kasa, when we would go to some of the villages, I would tie Eli on my back and off we would go on the one bicycle, sometimes 20 miles. We would often stay the night. There were no pampers at that time!! Later we got a motor bike but it was quite scary at times. Whenever big lorries would pass us on the main road it felt as if we would topple over.

In October 1976 our daughter Grace was born. She was just a few months old when we travelled on leave to the UK. During our leave we spoke in churches telling the Gwoza story through slide presentations and raising support for our Church work. Daniel did not know much English then so he would speak in Hausa and I would translate. Sometimes I would forget myself and turn to the people and speak to them in Hausa -- much to their amusement.

Although Daniel eventually learned to speak in English he always found it a challenge. However he speaks five of the eight Gwoza languages which are completely different from each other. Most of the time at home we communicate in Hausa and the girls know both languages. I find I very often think in Hausa and sometimes can't remember the English word!!

Later after having three girls and a hysterectomy the question among our Muslim friends was, "Why don't you take another wife as you have no boys?" Daniel reminded them that they heard our vows in Church that we stay together until death parts us. They were amazed as in their culture they would have taken more wives.

Eli and Grace were very much involved in our work. They would routinely give up their bed for a visitor or cook food for visitors after we had eaten. They both went to local schools wherever we worked. One day Grace came home and said she was not going back to school. She would just sell peanuts with some of the local women!! What had happened? It turned out that Grace knew more English than her teacher and she had pointed out some of his mistakes to him. This did not go down very well and she was caned for it. Eventually we sent her to my brother and sister-in- law's house in UK. Thankfully after one year she returned to join her sister in a Secondary School in Plateau State

We travelled on leave to UK on a second visit in 1983 with the girls. Our return was delayed because of a military coup that had taken place in Nigeria at the end of December. We were eventually given a place on the plane. We arrived on the tarmac at Kano International Airport only to meet soldiers with guns on either side of the steps. Welcome back to Nigeria!!

The Church had moved us to various other places and also two spells in Bible Colleges and then moved us back to Gwoza and we were there for 20 years before retirement. As you can see we were always busy and complimented each other very well. One of our main emphases was on the youth. Whenever our daughters were at home the young people were always in our compound playing table tennis or other games. At Christmas they used to go to different houses to celebrate. Years later we heard the youths would always come to our house first, as they knew we would cook a lot and have plenty of meat and special treats. They really enjoyed themselves.

In 2004 we reached the retirement age of 65 and retired from the Church work. But we were still very busy. In 2006 we accommodated young people from UK who came to Gwoza to help build a Computer School. Subsequently, many Christians and Moslems were trained in the Computer School and this helped to cement the good relationship between the two groups. In the same year a Clinic was also built and dedicated to Dr. Chandler and his wife, the pioneer missionaries in Gwoza. We enjoyed hosting two of their children who came from the UK and stayed with us.

While we lived in Gwoza, in 2004 a group called Taliban started in Bama, 50 miles from Gwoza, then moved to Gwoza town killing some people including security personnel and destroying some property. They then moved to Ngoshe Sama, one of the mountain villages, where the Nigerian army soldiers defeated them. A few times some of the youth in Gwoza would come to our street to burn our house down but the Moslem neighbours always protected us. Outside of the house was a big tree and the neighbours would meet there every day and whenever Daniel had time he would sit with them. This was why they respected us.

One day in 2011 some of the youths who were anti-Christian attacked the Church and Reverend's house and burnt some of the buildings. As it happened we were in Jos when this happened. They ran down the street from the Church to our house saying ours would be the next to be destroyed. Many of the youths tried to enter through the front gate. Two of them went around to the back wall and jumped over it. However they landed on a pile of zinc which made a lot of noise. This alerted the two young people who were inside looking after our house. The young people in our house looked for stones to throw at the intruders but all they could find was clay toys that the children on the compound had been making the previous day. They started to throw the clay pieces, but of course they couldn't see the intruders. Suddenly they heard one of the intruders say," Let's get out quickly as the *Baturya* will have guns hidden in the big water tank." Off they went with the others at the front gate and we were spared an attack.

In 2011 we moved to Daniel's village which was on the other side of the Gwoza Mountains near the Cameroon border. We built a new house on Daniels father's land.

In the meantime Boko Haram, the radical Islamism terrorist group, had grown stronger throughout Bornu State. By 2013 they were encroaching on territory around Gwoza and we were in danger. The British High Commissioner told me I must leave, so I went to UK. Boko Haram dressed as soldiers slaughtered hundreds of civilians in villages near Gwoza town including Daniel's village where we had settled. Boko Haram were burning houses near ours so Daniel reluctantly left his peoples and fled into the mountains with the young lad who lived on our Compound. While he was trying to climb the mountains behind our house, he fell into a hole and hurt his back. In the morning, before daybreak they came back to the house. As there was no medical help available our driver, who lived in the next village, brought him to Jos in our car. I returned to Nigeria a few weeks later in 2013 and joined Daniel in Jos in our daughter's house. Our house in the village was burnt down in June 2014 and we lost nearly everything but we were praising God we were alive.

When the Boko Haram occupied Gwoza and declared it their Caliphate in 2014 they killed Christians and Moslems who would not join them. However they didn't burn many houses and the Computer School building was saved, although all of the equipment was destroyed. When the Nigerian Army reoccupied Gwoza in 2015, the Computer School was renovated by *Doctors Without Borders.* They lived there and treated patients in the Government Hospital which had been taken over from the Mission Hospital in the early 70's. The Clinic was used as a Church when people started to return to Gwoza as all of the Churches had been destroyed. The Borno Government eventually rebuilt some of these Churches.

Meanwhile we started to receive phone calls from many of the

Gwoza people who were stranded on the Gwoza Mountains and needed help. Daniel advised them to try to come off the Gwoza mountains and cross the plains and climb the Cameroon mountains and make their way to places opposite Mubi or Yola and then cross back into Nigeria, get transport to Jos and come to us. So they started coming and before long we were looking after 35 families who had gradually found their way to Jos. They all had harrowing stories to tell of the attacks and their escape and Daniel became involved in counselling them as well as working to get them settled. I was engaged in getting people organised to cook food and thanks to support from our friends in UK we were able to settle the families in five different areas, with food, rented homes, bedding and kitchen equipment. Some have now settled elsewhere but we are still caring for 25 families. We moved to Vom, a village near Jos, and were given temporary accommodation in the Vom Hospital grounds in November 2016. We were able to build our own house in 2018 and now live comfortably among resettled Gwoza families in Vom. There are twenty five families in various areas and twenty widows that we are able to help. Also one hundred children now have UK sponsors. This keeps us busy with record-keeping and also being responsible for a block industry which we established to provide employment opportunities for some of the resettled families.

Let us tell you about our girls. Eli attended University and got a job as an art teacher at Hillcrest School in Jos. She was there for nearly 20 years before she died in her sleep in 2019. This was a great shock for everyone and she left a husband and three children. We were comforted by the fact that she had helped so many people. Grace also went to University and then later, in 2009, she and her husband settled in the UK. They have three children. Grace also helps and encourages many people. We have always had young people living with us and all 35 of them are part of our extended family.

I have always loved Gwoza and its people. So even though we were forced to leave, Gwoza is still very much a part of our life. Recently we celebrated 50 years of marriage and are now in our eighty's but we will carry on as long as we can to help our people.

DANIEL + KATHLEEN GULA
WITH ELI. 1974

A Politician's Wife

Sarah Chuwang

My Nigerian husband and I met as students at university in California. He obtained a Bachelors and Master's degrees in Political Science. After nine years in the United States, my father-in-law appealed to him to return to Nigeria. So in 1972 we came for a visit to Plateau State, my husband's home state. . While in Jos, the capital of Plateau State we met many influential personalities, including the late Military Governor of Benue-Plateau State, J. D. Gomwalk, and the late Gbong Gwom Jos. Both appealed to my husband to return to Nigeria and particularly to Jos in order to help build the State. Thus in 1975, we relocated to Nigeria from the United States.

I did not have many problems adjusting to my new life as my in-laws were ever ready to help me find my way around. Within a few months, I was employed by the Ministry for Social Welfare, and my husband was given a position in the Office of the Military Governor. The children were enrolled in school and also adjusted well. Initially, our lives were not significantly different from our lives in the US.

In May 1977, barely two years after we settled in Jos, my husband came home one day and informed me that he had quit his job and would contest for election into the National Constituent Assembly representing Jos. I was dumbfounded. I had many questions. If he won, would he move to Lagos, the capital city? How would we manage on one salary? Could I continue with my job, take care of two children and run a home in Nigeria all by myself? What would happen in an emergency? How would I be able to contact him? Lagos was far from home and telephone communication (over the landline) was uncertain and unreliable. Is this what was meant by "building the State"? Apprehension, uncertainly, and the realization I would become a politician's wife dawned on me for the first time because it had become obvious that my husband's passions was politics.

To his credit, my husband kept me informed of his campaign's progress, continued to support the family and continued to participate in visiting days at our children's schools. Additionally, he attended political meetings from dawn to dusk. I quickly learned that being a politician's wife meant many visitors, and they had to be entertained.

My husband won his election, and from October 1977 to September 1978, he sat as a Member of the Constituent Assembly. Although most Plateau Members came home once a month, they spent more time in consultations with colleagues than with their families.

Fortunately, I developed new interests and carved out a life for myself and the children while my husband was away. I made friends, learned to play golf and joined the Horticulture Society. During his time in Lagos, I also learned to deal with the usual inconveniences of living in a developing country. This period without my husband prepared me for what was to come later.

During my husband's time in the Assembly, I met many big name Second Republic politicians including Nnamdi Azikiwe, M.K.O. Abiola, Jim Nwobodo, Abubakar Rimi and Waziri Ibrahim. The politicians of that era were charismatic, but the one who stood out the most was Nnamdi Azikiwe (Zik). He exuded honesty, strength and a genuine love for Nigeria.

After the ban on political parties was lifted, my husband and other Plateau politicians got busy forming a political party named the Nigerian Peoples Party. It soon became clear to me that my husband's increased involvement in political activities would have a negative impact on our family life. One day my husband did not return home in the evening as usual. I did not want the children to worry so I told them their father had left early and come home after they had gone to bed. This went on for three days and three nights. They never knew their father had not come home at all and that I was very worried about him. Finally, in the early evening on the fourth day he arrived home. He explained that there had been a crisis in some states, and told me that he and a few others had to leave right away to keep the coalition intact. Needless to say, I was less than happy but I gave thanks to God that he was safe. This incident reinforced my need to become more self-sufficient, and make a normal life for my children. I now knew that until the elections took place, my husband was not my own.

During the elections, the Nigerian Peoples Party (NPP) won in Plateau State, and in August 1979 my husband was appointed Commissioner for Works and later Commissioner for Rural Development. Eventually life returned to normal, and my husband was able to strike a more equitable balance between his work and family life. He took up golf and we often played together. We had an active social life and the children liked their schools.

After serving in the Solomon Lar Administration for three years, my husband resigned from his appointment to contest for a seat in the House of Representatives representing Jos North. He knew it would be a hard fight judging by the composition of the Local Government, but he still wanted to give it a try. In September 1983 new elections were held; however, my husband did not win the seat and he began to rethink his future in politics.

Not long after the incoming administration took over in December 1983, the army staged a coup which ultimately led to General Muhammed Buhari becoming the Head of State. All democratic governmental institutions were dissolved and the Constitution suspended. This led to fifteen years of continuous military rule. Thus began my nightmare and the final process of discovering what it meant to be a politician's wife.

Within a week of the coup, a harsh message was broadcast on radio and television demanding all political office holders to report to the State Security Services (SSS). Initially we ignored the broadcast as my husband was not a political office holder. However, when the broadcasts became more threatening, he eventually reported to the SSS. He returned a short time later, accompanied by two officers who asked him to pack a few things for a day or two. They assured me there was nothing to worry about. The two or three days turned out to be nine months and eighteen days!

About one week after my husband was detained, the US Embassy contacted me stating that they were ready to lend assistance if necessary. Politicians and Heads of Agencies, both Federal and State, were detained. For some time no one knew where they had been detained and all we heard were rumours. There were rumours that they were in Jos Prison, Kirikiri Prison in Lagos or they had been moved to other States. Finally, to my relief I learned they were under detention in Jos at the Tudun Wada Government Lodge.

After several weeks my husband sent word for me to bring him his short-wave radio and some shaving foam. I immediately raced to the Lodge. As I was walking down the long driveway, a very young armed army officer shouted "Halt or I will shoot!" I kept on walking. When I got to the open gate, a senior officer came out and asked why I was there. I tried to explain my reason for approaching the Lodge, but before I could finish the young officer shouted again. I thought he would have a stroke! The senior officer told him to stand down, but he insisted that the radio I was holding could be used to contact foreign agents. I offered to surrender the radio for inspection. The senior officer said the radio was ok, but asked that I spray some of the shaving foam on my arm. Luckily when the detainees heard all the commotion, they came out onto a balcony to see what was happening. Fortunately, I was able to briefly identify my husband among the growing crowd.

Sometime later, the wife of another detainee came to my house to deliver some troubling news. She had been informed that the detainees had been moved to Lagos. So off we went back to the Lodge. The same scenario played out. "Halt or we will shoot!" We continued walking. The detainees came out and we spotted our husbands among them. Mission accomplished, and not a word had been spoken.

After about a two months' stay at the Lodge, the detainees were moved to Jos Prison. Fortunately for me, the Controller was a friend and he called to assure me that my husband was safe and nothing would happen to him. He also urged me to call him whenever I felt the need. `I will forever be indebted to the Controller. He was one of the few men of integrity who later resigned his job with the prison service rather than make life difficult for the detainees.

The detainees had their own section in the prison and could buy their own food. In addition, some prisoners were reassigned to cook and take care of them. The detainees even contributed money and bought a ping pong table. For Easter, I made up a basket containing fruits, sweets, drinks and a cake. This had been sanctioned by the Controller; however, the gateman insisted I cut the cake. I refused, and he commented about the *bature* (foreign) woman always "disturbing" them.

For several months I hid from my children the fact that their father was in prison. However, one day while I was preparing to take some things to my husband, my son said he would go out with me. Not thinking, I told him he did not want to go to the prison. He yelled, "You mean Dad is behind bars!" I was forced to explain the situation, and from that moment onward my son's respect for Nigerian Government was gone. That disdain continues to this day.

Rumours continued to fly that the detainees were being moved to Lagos. It seemed every dishonest person, including some that I thought were friends, offered to forestall the move and/or secure my husband's release, but for a <u>price</u>.! All the wives of detainees received such visits. These visits began to take their toll on me until eventually I came to the realization that I was powerless to change the situation. At last, after about six months, the visits stopped and my husband remained in Jos.

Early during the detention period, I received visits three times by SSS officers and an Indian structural engineer. On the first visit, the officers searched every nook and cranny of the house, while the engineer demanded to see structural drawings, architectural drawings and the site plan of our house. He also tapped on the walls and floors and seemed confused and the officers were disappointed. They had expected to find stashes of cash and hidden rooms. During the second visit, the officers searched more thoroughly. Even my children's bedrooms, closets and drawers were inspected. The search of my children's private spaces was most upsetting since we had always afforded them a certain level of privacy and independence. On the third visit, I refused them entrance and ordered them off my property. My tone of voice and level of speech left them with no doubt I meant it. I later learned they had received an anonymous tip that the house was built on an island and that there was a secret room with many cars. The house was actually in the middle of the Government Residential Area (GRA) and was surrounded on all sides by other homes.

I was also the subject of an investigation about two years prior to the coup. For many years I owned a bookstore specializing in professional books, children's books and toys. I had a contract from the Ministry of Education to supply a large number of children's books that would eventually be distributed to State primary schools. When I supplied the books, the stores' officer verified receipt of the order but refused to sign the delivery note. I knew what he wanted, refused to comply and left his office. Immediately I went to my husband's office, got his aide-de-camp and both of us went back to discuss the matter further. Once the stores' officer realized who I was, he accused me of trying to get him fired, but begrudgingly signed the delivery note. Later during my husband's detention, I got a summons from the Special Investigation Panel (SIP) to answer some questions regarding the children's books order. I was concerned about the possibility my being detained. I said to myself, they have the father, and now they want the mother!, I arranged for my son's godmother to pick him up from school if I didn't come back before 5pm. Fortunately, I had all the documents, including the award of contract, payment voucher and the all-important delivery note. I had made packets for each panel member. After inspecting my documents, they thanked me for my thoroughness and dismissed me. Other business people were not as fortunate and were forced to refund the money after providing similar services.

As a consequence of being subjected to uncertain and extremely stressful conditions several detainees, including my husband, developed high blood pressure and were hospitalized. I had been told that the Plateau State Military Administrator was one of the most wicked individuals to serve in that capacity. Sadly, he was a "brother", a fellow Plateau man. When the Plateau State Administrator learned that some of the detainees had been allowed to be hospitalised he ordered the Chief Medical Director to discharge the detainees immediately or else he, being a foreign national, would be deported. The detainees were discharged, but the Chief Medical Director was permitted to treat them on an outpatient basis. This ended up being a blessing in disguise. The prison, the hospital and my store were all within walking distance of each other. The SSS minders allowed the detainees to visit my store, and they quickly turned it into the meeting place for themselves and their wives. There was much joy, laughter and kisses. On some days, you could hardly find a place to stand. Wives from across the country heard about what was going on, and I gladly offered them hospitality. The downside was that it came with a cost to me. The SSS minders routinely "asked for" and were given items from the store. They loved Parker Pens, bestseller books and children's toys. It was worth what I was losing. I am sure the State Military Administrator knew what was going on but he did not interfere. However, he wanted stricter prison conditions placed on the detainees which the Controller refused to do and he resigned his job.

As the saying goes, "everything that has a beginning has an ending". On December 31, 1983, General Ibrahim Babangida staged a coup and placed Buhari in detention. Unbeknown to me, he ordered the release of all detainees, and my husband telephoned me asking me to pick him up. He emerged wearing a suit and tie, suitcase in one hand and his pillow under his arm.

After his release, my husband refused to work with the military in any capacity. Thus ended my years as a politician's wife. I would never wish for any other woman to experience life as the wife of a detained politician. Once Military Rule ended, he mentored many aspirants for elective office and served on various screening committees and boards.

After that tumultuous period, I ran Windows of the World, an interior-decoration business, for nineteen years and was the Chairman of All Farmers Association of Nigeria (AFAN) Plateau State Chapter for thirteen years.

Most my experiences in this country have not been as traumatic. For example, while I was running Windows of the World, I made extensive use of our famously hazardous roads. I have also enjoyed the beauty of the countryside and hospitality of the people I have met along the way. I have even experienced what it like to travel via the "night bus" to Aba in South Eastern Nigeria to purchase materials for curtains.

The bus leaves Jos about 6:00pm daily and arrives in Aba in the early hours of the following morning. At the start of the journey every regular fare -paying passenger has a comfortable assigned seat. Shortly after leaving the bus station a "fire and brimstone" preacher starts sermonizing to a captive audience. When the passengers are finally "left in peace", the driver drops him off at a pre-arranged location. At the same stop, on hops a native medicine seller. He has a bag full of all kinds of concoctions and promises they will heal everything from erectile dysfunction to mental illness. He walks up and down the aisle for about thirty minutes trying to sell his wonder drugs Again, at a pre-arranged location the driver pulls over and off goes the medicine seller goes. Suddenly from nowhere, a rush of people board the bus and simultaneously a number of small wooden stools miraculously appear. These stools are for the *attaches* or "attachments". *Attaches* typically pay less than the regular fare, and are actually illegal extra passengers who pay the driver through the conductor of the bus. Once the *attaches* are seated on their stools placed throughout the middle of the aisle, every other available space is taken up by those who choose to stand for the entire journey. They too pay a lower unofficial fare for that privilege. If you think you can finally get some sleep, then you are wrong. That's when at least one very loud argument breaks out. Usually, these arguments are about encroaching on another passenger's personal space and last for about fifteen minutes. No one, including the conductor intervenes. After ten hours we reach the intended destination – Aba. The driver makes periodic hazardous stops on the way to the bus garage, dropping a few passengers at a time. This practice helps passengers reach their final destinations sooner at less cost. The bus ultimately comes to a stop in the garage, and all remaining passengers disembark. I am usually part of the "early disembark" crowd and proceed to check into a hotel and take a quick shower. After eating a much-needed breakfast, I set off to the market.

Day one at the market involves heading to the store of a particular "customer" (aka vendor as they say in Nigeria) from whom I regularly purchase fabrics. He was always really nice to me. Any subsequent purchases from other customers in the market would be carried to his shop and packed in bales for me by his hired hands who were experts in packing. He would even make arrangements to deliver my purchases to the bus garage prior to my return journey.

Day two involves making a return visit to purchase additional items. Aba is so hot and humid it feels like living in an oven. Frozen water packs are the only source of relief while bargaining for the transportation of my goods back to Jos. That exercise usually takes at least an hour of serious haggling. Day two ends with the return journey back to Jos, which pretty much follows the same pattern as day one: getting on the bus, a preacher, a medicine seller, and arguments and so on.

Over the years, I have learned a lot about the character of Nigerians from while travelling via the night-bus. They are willing to suffer a lot of stress and inconvenience to save a few Naira. It might mean sitting on a very low stool or standing all the way for ten hours. No opportunity to make money should be lost. It might also mean selling your concoctions on a moving bus. Not every argument resulted in a physical altercation or required intervention. Nigerians have a great deal of respect for women in distress and will make sacrifices for them. They are great business men and women and will go out of their way to build customer loyalty.

During one of my trips, with my daughter in tow, the bus broke down in the middle of nowhere late into the night. We were told not to worry, and that another bus would be arriving soon to take us to Aba. After getting off the bus, we stood a fair distance from the other passengers and hoped seats would be available when other bus arrived. After an hour, the bus pulled up and stopped directly in front of me. Two strong arms extended from the bus door and pulled both of us into the already full bus. We were the first to enter. Once inside the bus, we discovered those strong arms belonged to a Jos acquaintance of mine. Another acquaintance gave up his seat to me, and a generous *attache* gave his stool to my daughter!

I think my children have been privileged being equally Nigerian and American. My two sons live and work in the US, and often say having "survived" boarding school in Nigeria they can endure anything. They have witnessed real poverty, flawed political systems, true friendships across national and geographical boundaries and the value of not only family life but extended family connections. These experiences have made them more than equipped to live more fulfilling lives. Our younger son is more connected to Nigeria as he was a toddler when his father was detained. The older son has never gotten over his father's detention in Nigeria. My daughter is 100% Nigerian although she was 11 years old when we moved to Nigeria. She lives in Jos and is more comfortable in Nigeria than in America.

My husband of 52 years has passed away. Because of this there has been much speculation about whether or not I would stay in Nigeria. Yes indeed, I worry about the lack of security, lack of consistent electricity and water supply and other concerns. But the people in my life are MORE important. Nigeria has offered me many cherished opportunities such as the ability to host a TV program, serve as a member on multiple governmental bodies and represent Plateau State at multiple international agricultural conferences. I have had the pleasure of being elected to serve on numerous organizations (sometimes in leadership roles). I even have received several horticultural awards from the British Royal Horticultural Society. None of this would be possible had I remained in the US. People forget or are unaware of the fact that I have lived in Nigeria far far far longer than I lived in America. I have great friends, creature comforts, a loving daughter, grandsons, extended family and a robust support system. What more could I ask for?

That Stuff

Megan Olusanya

My first day in Nigeria was very exciting for me. The year was 1964. I had grown up in Jamaica and worked in Ontario, Canada where I met my husband. We had arrived Lagos at 4 a.m. that morning and now I was in the home of my mother-in-law. We met many relatives of my husband. Most of them did not speak English and spoke in their language which was Yoruba. Since I never heard a different language before, their conversation sounded as if they were having a heated argument and I felt lost. But I was welcomed.

At lunch time I ate a very tasty dish which was prepared by my Mother-in-law and her helpers. I asked my husband what was the dish and he told me it was made from yam and accompanied with a vegetable stew. The yam was very smooth and made into a ball. I thought that the yam was made into a flour for it to be so smooth!

On the following day when my husband was away, I was asked what would I like to eat for lunch I quickly said 'yam flour' meaning the same thing I ate the day before!

When my husband returned, we sat at the table and the food was brought. I saw something wrapped neatly with green leaves and it had a funny odor. I informed my husband that I did not want to eat 'that stuff'. He called his Mother who told him that I had specifically requested for that dish! I started crying, saying that I could not have asked for that dish when I did not even know what it was! There was a big commotion as his mother and all the helpers were insisting that I asked for that specific dish. My husband then said, 'I think there is a problem of communication here'. Can you imagine how I felt when I was told that the yam that was served the day before was 'pounded' and that what I asked for was 'yam flour' which was yam prepared in an entirely different way and called 'amala'! I apologized to my mother-in-law. I have never tasted 'amala' ever since!

This was the first out of many encounters with a Nigerian situation and one that I never forgot!!!

This was taken the day of my story. The outfit was waiting for me
when I came and it was the first time my mother-in-law dressed me

From Northern Ireland to Nigeria:
The Landscape of Memory

Elizabeth Brown-Peterside

I was born in County Down, Northern Ireland and grew up there in a very small market "town" where my father had a hardware business. Everybody knew each other and it was perfectly safe for us children to roam all around completely unsupervised. I went to the Protestant school which had four teachers; the Catholics had their own separate school. Apart from the fact that there were two separate schools, there was no tension that I was aware of between us. For secondary school, I travelled by bus to Newry Grammar school for three years, and then to boarding school at Princess Gardens, just outside Belfast. After that, I proceeded to Queen's University, Belfast and got a B.A. degree, followed by one year at teacher training. Finally, in 1953 I started teaching.

While growing up, I had dreams of going to the USA to visit my Aunt Ruby, who lived in Rhode Island, so I started saving money for the trip. Finally, in 1958, I got a chance to travel to the USA with a fellow teacher. We travelled down to Cork and set sail and I really enjoyed visiting my cousins. Nine weeks later, we travelled back on the Queen Mary and that was when I met my future husband, Galbraith (known as Gally), Brown-Peterside. It was a shipboard romance that lasted over 40 years.

My Nigerian husband-to-be had been in the USA attending several colleges for about eight years (obtaining a BA in Political Science and a MA in Public Administration) but decided to study law and become a barrister. As Nigeria followed British law, he felt he ought to study in London and go the Inns of Court where he'd got admission at Middle Temple. We met on the ship at a game of table tennis. I was playing table tennis and a group of young Black men came along the deck and started talking to us. I don't remember the details but by the end of the voyage the two of us had become friends and decided to keep in touch. I returned to Belfast, but I remember exchanging a few letters and also visiting London over the following months.

The result was that we got married in April, 1959 but very quietly in a registry office in London. I had already been a bridesmaid and an important guest at another wedding, but we only had eight people present at ours. It was, of course, on account of the 'colour problem'. I knew that many of my relatives would not attend the wedding and my husband knew very few people. Only my brother and sister-in-law came from my side. Two of Gally's friends joined us. Dike was from the present Rivers State like my husband who was from Opobo but was brought up in Jos.

In our first year of marriage, my husband, as a law student ate his dinners at Middle Tempe and I taught at Swaffield School, South London and then at St. Leonard's School, Streatham. Our first child, a daughter, was born in 1960, my husband was called to the bar in November 1961, and in early February 1962, we took the train to Liverpool and set sail for Lagos. The heat and humidity in Lagos were completely over-powering. I'll never forget that day we arrived, chasing after my daughter and being five months pregnant, sweating constantly with no relief. There was no air conditioning then. Still, we had a great time in Lagos. We stayed in a nice, airy house in Ikoyi with a couple from the North who my husband knew. We also had two cordial rather formal welcomes from family members.

After ten days in Lagos, we left for Aba in the Eastern Region, where my father-in-law was then living. He was a retired teacher. After his formal training, he had been posted to the Northern Region, Jos, to be precise, and had to learn the local language, Hausa. He did so and got 98% in his final exam. When I met him, I found he spoke perfect, beautifully accented English too. He was a native of Opobo, an island in the Niger Delta. The journey to Aba was by car and took about eighteen hours. I only remember it was very long and very hot and we bought lots of oranges. They were all peeled in a way I had never seen before, with just a thin layer of skin peeled off all over, leaving a "white" orange, and then you sucked out the juice from the top. Delicious.

We finally arrived at a modern little house in Aba, and very quickly, a little camp bed was put up for me and my daughter and we soon fell fast asleep. The house had electricity but no running water. There was an outside "bathroom" or bathing room. Next morning, I was shown the bathroom where a bucket of water was waiting. I closed the door and saw there was a small drain for the water to run off. I never did enjoy a bath more than that one, getting rid of the previous day's sweat and orange juice. And to this day, I still have a bucket bath!

Very soon afterwards, my father-in-law paid two months' rent for us for a flat in a brand-new modern apartment block So my husband made arrangements to start up his own private law practice. The weather was very hot and humid and I developed a lot of boils and a skin complaint which produced excruciatingly itchy, red blotches on my arms and legs.

I was very keen to learn to cook Nigerian food, so my husband organized several wives of his colleagues to come and teach me. I watched carefully and wrote out the recipes and soon I was able to cook egusi and okra soups, yam pottage, and jollof rice. I wanted my children to eat and come to love Nigerian food.

Meanwhile my friend, Judy, who was now living in Port Harcourt, came and visited me. She was able to recommend Shell company facilities in Port Harcourt and a Catholic hospital in Anua, not too far from Ikot Ekpenne in the opposite direction for the birth of my second baby. The Shell hospital was very expensive so I went to investigate Anua, well over an hour's drive away. I remember standing in line – it was so hot and steamy – I wore a wrapper gathered above my chest with my shoulders bare. This made it somewhat more comfortable.

On May 28, 1962, my husband took me back to Anua and our first son was born. That day, to get to Aba, we passed through Ikot Ekpenne which I will always remember as it had lots of raffia mats for sale. The hospital in Anua was a mere dot in the bush and they had mosquito nets over the beds. I loved sleeping under mosquito nets. I felt very safe and snug under them. The hospital was well run by nuns, the

Medical Missionaries of Mary. There were no men at all as the establishment was entirely run by women. I understand that now it has become a large government hospital.

So, we settled down to life in Aba. I nursed my son for several months, and stayed at home all that year. When he was old enough, my baby son used to jig up and down around 5 am to the sound of trains passing nearby. In January 1963, I found a teaching job at Sacred Heart College on Owerri Road, quite near where we lived. It was a Boy's Secondary School. The headmaster was Father Smith. The students were very respectful, but I remember the geckos running up and down the bare walls behind me. There were other expatriates there and I became good friends with Mrs Betty Kirk. She took me to Port Harcourt several times for shopping and I found the car journey so strange. The road had been cut out of the flat bush or forest and all one could see going along the edge of the nice paved road were very tired-looking faded palm trees, so different to the mountains and green rolling hills of Ireland.

My husband didn't seem to be making much progress with his law practice. Certainly, there were others, sons of the soil, who had returned to Aba from overseas and there was a lot of competition. So, the decision was made that we move to Jos. My father-in-law was well acquainted with Northern Nigeria and recommended that we relocate to Jos, which he described as being "cold."

Gally was a real 'Northerner' through his mother who was a Fulani woman from the Nigeria/Cameroon border. She had come to Jos while fleeing an arranged marriage in her village. The southern teacher (my father-in-law) from Opobo saw her selling *fura da nono* (milk and curds) by the roadside. He was smitten by this Fulani milkmaid, and soon after they were married. Unfortunately, she died before I arrived on the scene but her uncles and other relatives were well known to us. Gally's parents had been married for some years and had three children, but when my father-in-law was transferred back to the South, to Aba, his Fulani wife did not accompany him. The one family member my husband was very close to was his sister, Iris, who became known to us as Hajiya as she was Muslim and went to Mecca more than once. The third sibling, a brother, died young. Hajiya lived in Maiduguri in the north east with her two sons but later moved to Jos and lived on our compound before she got her own place in town. She ran a restaurant in Jos so we always had close contact with her sons and all the young people who worked for her. My husband, apparently was made fun of and called a 'Hausa boy' by the southern branch of the family in Opobo. There were family tensions on account of my father-in-law's marriage to the Fulani woman.

We packed up and moved to Jos in May 1964. We travelled in a small Volkswagen, my husband driving, me in the front, with my son's nurse maid in the back with our daughter. The "road" was a rough track, stony, and there were so many rickety wooden bridges, I often feared we would tumble into the water below, but we got to Makurdi safely. We stayed the night there before continuing our journey to Jos the following day. That road was mostly uphill and there were fewer trees as we climbed up the Jos Plateau. As we came nearer to Jos, the land was fairly flat and open and grassy with huge clusters of rocks from time to time. It was spectacular in a different kind of way and so different from those tired palm trees around Aba.

The first flat we lived in was in a very pleasant and quiet area, mid-way between two hospitals, Our Lady of Apostles (OLA) which was Catholic and Evangel, run by American missionaries. We had rented the flat from a lady in our block in Aba, who had previously lived in Jos. It was part of a longer terrace, but this one had an extra little "lodge" and it became my husband's office. But soon my husband felt it was too far out of the centre of town and so we moved to the main commercial area above a bank. Just behind us was a bakery run by a Lebanese couple and so I discovered "flat bread". Ahmadu Bello Way, the street we lived on, was quite busy with many Lebanese gentlemen trading in cloth. I particularly remember the name AB Chami. There was a shop with fancy goods of all kinds run by an Indian, Mr Salawni, and Chellerams and Chanrai supplied all of our food. We also had Bata Shoe Shop and Leonards, both for shoes. There was one major shop on that street run by Nigerians, the Akanji family. Mr Akanji sat by the till at the door all the time and was friendly, though he had quite an intimidating presence. Sadly, his wife. died some years later in a car accident. Finally on May 28, 1969, my first son's 7th birthday, we moved into our own house in the Government Residential Area (GRA). In time, my husband built his office there too.

Those early years in Jos were very interesting, with both happy and sad occasions. Our second daughter was born in 1964 and later that year I went to teach at St Murumba College, a secondary school for boys. It was near our house, out on the untarred section of Zaria Road and the short journey always reminded me of "cowboy country". There were no buildings along the main road then, just two or three lanes leading off with buildings visible at the end of them. The scenery was rocky and sandy and brown and bare. Father O'Connor was the principal and very hospitable. St Murumba's was built to accommodate boys from the Middle Belt and the South as the few government schools at the time favoured boys from the real Hausa-speaking North, so we had Igbo Yoruba, Idoma and Tiv students. I left at the end of 1965 and several months later, my third daughter was born. Sometime after this my four-year old son broke his leg and was in OLA for many weeks while it was healing. Then in May 1967, our second son was born. A month later my oldest daughter was badly burned in a domestic fire accident. It was early night time, there was an electricity cut which was fairly common in Jos and we were using candles. The two younger children were asleep. I left my oldest daughter and son and went around to the other side of the house to feed the baby. Shortly afterwards, my daughter came running and screaming with her pyjama top on fire. She sustained third degree burns on her upper chest and back and it was many months before they healed, leaving severe scars.

My mother came from Ireland to visit the following year, and was delayed in going back because her home was flooded with water up to eighteen inches, so she was still with us at Christmas. Late on Boxing Day, my toddler son began to choke seriously all of a sudden. I think he started to cry while eating a biscuit and inhaled a piece of it. My husband and I rushed him to Bingham Hospital, but he died a few days later. It was a very sad time for us.

Evangel Hospital, run by SIM missionaries, was very close to where we lived and was the scene of a lot of drama. In 1969, Lassa Fever, a new disease emerged in Lassa, a village in north eastern Nigeria, and made its way to Jos. In fact, Dr. Janette Troup, whom we knew well, died from it, after she cut her finger while doing a post-mortem. She was so well known and loved, and had worked in Jos for many year. it was such a cruel blow. However, Nurse Penny Pinneo, who also contracted Lassa fever, survived and was able to return to the United States. Both of these women had cared for my toddler son at Bingham Hospital.

All this time, my husband was working very hard and often went on long journeys to Maidugari, Yola, Makurdi, Gombe, Bauchi and

Kafanchan –all over the North, which was one big region in those days. He absolutely loved the law and worked with great joy and enthusiasm, covering a huge variety of cases, from litigation to criminal defence, some of which are featured in the Nigeria Law Reports. His passion and hard work paid off as in 1982, he was selected to become an S.A.N., Senior Advocate of Nigeria, the Nigerian equivalent of a QC in England. He was thrilled and we were so proud of him, the first SAN in Plateau State.

We discovered St. Piran's Church-on-the Plateau where the services were in English. (The church closest to us at the time was Igbo speaking.) I went to there with my then four-year-old daughter to explore one Sunday in 1964. It was a tiny Anglican church with at least one stained glass window and a plaque which said the Queen had worshipped there in 1953. There were only seven or eight people in church including three children, all white, but the preacher that day was Nigerian. I later learned that the preacher was Mr. Peter Gowon, a lay reader in the Anglican Church. Peter Gowon's younger brother, Yakubu, later became the Head of State in Nigeria and we got to know Peter's family well. I learned that this expatriate community had built this church and had their own compounds at Rayfield and Barkin Ladi, villages outside Jos. They had come to the Jos area to mine tin. They also set up their own primary schools for their children. To us, wives of Nigerians, it seemed the expatriates had pleasant, easy lives with all sorts of perks. Their older children went off to boarding schools in the UK, with all their fees paid for until they were eighteen. But in time, the expatriates left Jos as more and more states were created and St. Piran's church, named for the patron saint of tin miners, grew and grew and is now filled with Nigerians. The present building is the fourth edition of St Piran's-on-the-Plateau, and the plaque about the Queen visiting is still there.

We sent our children to Hillcrest School, run by missionaries, a 10-minute walk from our home. It was a place of many happy hours. I loved singing the Messiah in their community choir for many years even after four of our children had graduated from the school. Because the school followed an American curriculum, our children had to attend college in the US. The youngest, a son born three years after the son that died, completed his education in the UK. Also, our youngest daughter moved to London from the US and trained to be an osteopath.

Through an American friend, I became acquainted with the association called Nigerwives. Two ladies came from Lagos came to explain to us what the association was all about. It is an organization of foreign wives from all over the world brought together through marriage to Nigerian men. We thought it a very good idea and soon started up our own branch in Jos. The meetings and social gatherings were most enjoyable. I loved getting to know the ladies from countries as far afield as Indonesia and Jamaica, Russia and Australia. I even remember a lady from St. Helena, the island in the middle of the Atlantic, where Napoleon went!

Early Jos life was so good that I stayed there thirty eight years, and I lived forty years altogether in Nigeria. My husband died in 1999 after a brief illness and I returned to the UK in 2002, choosing to settle in London where I had spent my early years as a young wife. Jos was a lovely place and I was very happy there. And our family home there, is still going strong. My younger son is busy renovating the place, and my daughter, the osteopath, lives there with her two children and is now working in her father's office where she has a clinic.

When growing up in that small market town in Northern Ireland, I never could have imagined I'd have such a fascinating life.

Soft Drinks

Kanchana Ugbabe

The coloured bottles of Coca Cola, Fanta and Sprite were quite a novelty to me when I first arrived in Zaria, Nigeria in 1975 and set up house with my Nigerian husband. On our way from Kano International airport, one of the billboards that caught my attention said, 'Things go better with Coke. In India where I grew up we offered coffee to visitors in stainless steel tumblers. Fresh, aromatic, sweet, milky coffee frothing at the top of the tumbler. Even children were accustomed to drinking coffee. The story goes of how as a six year old, I scandalously demanded coffee while visiting a relative's home. We had been served fried savoury snacks and *ladoos*. My young cousins who accompanied me sat demurely, apparently showing little interest in what had been set before us. I dived into the snacks and *ladoos* and then proceeded to ask, 'Is there no coffee?' I can't remember how my mother dealt with the faux pas afterwards but I don't think I got taken out visiting again!

Buying soft drinks in crates was something I had never done before. When my husband brought a crate of mineral drinks and cartons of beer and kept them for visitors my pantry looked like a corner store .I arranged the bottles on the pantry shelf because they looked so pretty. When we visited our neighbours or my husband's friends, we were offered the coloured bottles. A glass accompanied it sometimes. At other times we drank it straight out of the bottle. The aerated drinks always left me feeling bloated in the stomach somewhat, but I was gradually getting used to

When I was still a new arrival in Nigeria, whenever visitors came to our home, I would bring the coloured bottles out of the pantry and lined them up on the coffee table as soon as they sat down. After the initial greetings they would open up the bottles and drink and watch the News on television. I didn't have to entertain them as such or keep elaborate conversation going. When they had sat long enough, they would thank me for the drinks and leave. My mother in law who was with us at that time watched grimly. I was trying to impress her with my cultural adjustments.

After a couple of months Mama said to me one day that I would reduce my husband to poverty if I served drinks to everyone so readily and elaborately. She said I had to use my discretion. "Sometimes, you tell the visitor you had just run out of drinks and that you were planning on buying a crate when they arrived! Entertain them with your mouth,"she said. "Tell them they are most welcome and that they must come again. " A sweet mouth, as they say in Nigeria.

I let my husband handle the coloured bottles after that. He added Johnny Walker's whiskey to it and red wine sometimes. Or the visitors drank beer out of giant green bottles. My mother in law said nothing.

Engaging in a New World in Ile-Ife

Jane Oshinowo

My journey to Nigeria started in the early 1960s. This was the era of African independence. My parents were caught up in the excitement of the times and became involved with the African Student Foundation (ASF) which awarded scholarships to African students to study at Canadian universities. My parents welcomed African students to our home. There were enjoyable evenings with animated discussion and music. Two Nigerian women students, at different times, lived with us during the academic year. My mother kept in contact with some of these students many years beyond their graduation. In 1964 I was home for the holidays just in time for the ASF Christmas party. My mother encouraged me to attend the party. There I was to meet my future husband. We dated for a few months and went our separate ways. Sometime later I met him at a party at the International Students Centre in Toronto. This time our relationship resulted in marriage which my parents supported. My father was satisfied after asking my husband-to -be about polygamy. His response was that I would always be his first wife.

Our first few years of marriage were very busy with my husband completing his PhD and starting work with a Toronto firm; I also worked between giving birth and caring for our two sons. During these early years my husband spent some time teaching me some Yoruba words and Yoruba cooking. Then we received news that my mother-in-law had had a stroke. We flew to Nigeria to visit her. During the visit we came to the decision that now was the time to move to Nigeria. My husband explored employment opportunities and was offered a position at the University of Ife. With these plans in place we returned to Toronto to prepare for the move. I was preparing with the intent to spend the rest of my life with my husband in Nigeria.

My husband, two sons, and I had arrived in Lagos in January 1974 leaving a winter landscape in Toronto. As we were driven from the airport I was taking in the congestion, and the 'chaos' of a densely populated city deficient in infrastructure .The tropical heat hit me powerfully as it was just a few days earlier that we had been ice skating. Driving through the city it was disturbing to see a victim of violence lying by the side of the road. The war had ended just a couple of years prior to our arrival. Although the conflagration did not reach Lagos, the war reached in other ways as seen by the abandoned deceased. As well it was a bit unnerving to see groups of armed soldiers performing policing duties. It was a lot for me to take in. But shortly we arrived at my sister-in-law's home where we enjoyed a warm welcome by the family we would live with for the next three months.

My husband left for Ife to start work as a lecturer at the University of Ife while the boys and I stayed behind with my sister-in-law and her family. It was great that they had two sons close in age to our two sons. The boys forged a strong bond playing together. It was the beginning of a wonderful relationship. It also provided a crash course in Yoruba family life and how to live in a tropical country. At first I felt incompetent as a woman in this new milieu. Without my sister-in-law my transition from Canada to Nigeria would have been so much harder. She was an amazing woman, a community and church leader, and a midwife who managed her private maternity centre. Sister Bose was welcoming and supportive, never critical. I always looked forward to staying with Sister Bose during our frequent visits to Lagos. Since many of my husband's family lived in or near Lagos we visited often over the years to attend family events establishing strong relationships with other siblings. Yoruba society is polygamous so my husband had many half siblings, and it took many visits to Lagos before I could place individuals on the family tree.

Finally we were all headed to Ile- Ife, the cradle of Yoruba civilization, to settle in to a new life. The entrance to the University of Ife was impressive having a gateway and a long dual carriageway to face Oduduwa Hall, a beautiful architectural building. At that time the University of Ife was a young university, being just over 10 years old when I arrived. The well laid out university encompassed 25 square miles with a sports centre, student housing, academic buildings, staff club, senior staff housing, research farm, commercial farm, a supermarket and a small zoo that was latter shut down. Not only was the University rich in its' physical resources, it was also rich in its human resources with academic staff from the international community and from across southern Nigeria. The Vice-Chancellor was a tall impressive Yoruba man who was very welcoming to his new academic staff. The faculties were growing. My husband was one of many Nigerian academics filling the new positions. It was exciting for me. I was happy for my husband and proud of him.

Unfortunately the house we had been assigned was not yet ready so we stayed with my husband's cousin, his wife, and their four children. Again this was a wonderful opportunity for us to develop a family relationship in Ife. They generously accommodated us for a month.

Our assigned house was an attached bungalow in Kosile Estate, a short street on the edge of town with about 20 homes built to accommodate university staff. With some help, my husband hired a "house boy" and negotiated the terms of his employment. Our house boy lived with us in his own separate quarters. I never did become comfortable with having a house boy, but I appreciated his work. A very important job for our house boy was to carry buckets of water from the tank to our house when there was no water in the taps. Also as we settled into the week-day routine of work and school I found it helpful to have an extra pair of hands and someone to stay with boys after I started working. My husband would pick up the boys from school and bring them home for lunch. They enjoyed school. The boys quickly made friends and enjoyed playing with them on the street. As a family we ate breakfast and supper together. Evenings were family time, but that did not continue after our move to campus a few years later. On weekends we socialized with friends, often spending the afternoons relaxing and swimming at the staff club. Our older son was bold and learned how to swim, dive and flip as he played with other children. Our younger son was more hesitant but learned to swim when left to his own pace. There were no organized swimming lessons. There were frequent parties at friends' homes celebrating some milestone. Sometimes we went to movies or other cultural events at Oduduwa hall.

My husband was the oldest male of his mother, sister Bose being the eldest of eight full siblings. Being married to the oldest son, I was considered the first wife in the family – the first woman to marry into this family. Although there was an older married half sibling, he and his wife were living abroad, thus the responsibility of being the first wife fell on me. The first occasion in which I had to take on this responsibility was during the marriage of my husband's younger brother. Being new to the country, I had not had any opportunity to get to know the bride, so I felt somewhat uncomfortable performing my expected duties. The traditional part of the wedding I participated in involved some of the family wives, female family members and a male family member going to the bride's family compound to bring the new wife to her husband's home. The occasion involved an introduction with greetings in several different languages. Then the groom's entourage asks for the family to bring out the bride. After a few different women are presented and denied, the bride is finally brought out. She is greeted with much joy. Songs, both traditional and religious are sung and prayers are bestowed on the bride. Sometimes the bride's family will keep the groom's family waiting, as if they did not want to give up the bride. It is a joyful occasion, both fun and solemn. At the end of the ceremony we brought the new wife, my new sister-in-law, to her husband's family compound. At the family house, in welcoming the new wife I washed her feet and escorted her upstairs to be welcomed by her new family. More blessings were bestowed on the bride and groom. Only then did the new couple join in the celebration. The party continued until the early hours with music and dancing. As the adults partied, the children played together, our sons thoroughly enjoying themselves, until sleep caught up with them.

After settling into our assigned home on Kosile Estate I was fortunate to obtain a position of Ward Sister at the Seventh-Day Adventist Hospital in Ife. Our two boys were enrolled in the Staff primary school on the university campus. This was a new experience for both our sons as they had never been in a classroom as they had gone to a Montessori school for preschool learning. Fortunately they both adjusted very well. I worked from 8am to 5pm Monday to Friday. My husband would first drop me at work and then take the boys to school before going to work himself. There was very limited public transport, thus I had to depend on my husband to get to and from work. Grocery shopping was done at the local market, going from stall to stall, seller to seller to purchase such items as palm oil, gari, yam tubers, yam flour, beans etc. Transactions were done in Yoruba. Initially my husband was supportive, teaching me the rudimentary marketplace Yoruba so that I could shop without his assistance. I enjoyed going to the market, greeting my 'customers' as they greeted me with 'our wife' or oyinbo. As we had one car we had to work together, but I was very dependent on him. He showed me around the university campus, his office and department, and in town businesses such as the bank, and car mechanic's workshop. Everything was new to me and I embraced it all, sometimes with trepidation.

Learning the Yoruba language was important to me so I could be more a part of the community. I had hoped that my husband would help me by speaking the language at home. However he would not speak to me or to our sons in Yoruba. I was unhappy about this as I struggled to improve my command of the language over the many years. I did not seek out someone to instruct me in the language but relied on colleagues. Several years later, an English woman who had earned a PhD in Yoruba language developed and conducted a course in Yoruba as a second language. The class, held weekly for 6 weeks, comprised of various non-Yoruba members of the University community. This course was very helpful to me in improving my communication skills in Yoruba. English is the official language in Nigeria so that communication at work and school was in English; however in social and family situations people spoke in Yoruba. At work most patients did not speak English so with help from my colleagues I was able to communicate basically with my patients, which sometimes could have both of us laughing.

At Kosile estate my husband and I tried our hands at farming, planting yam, corn and okra. The land was fairly fertile so we were able to enjoy the fruits of our labour. A few years later at our new staff house we planted some trees and shrubs such as frangipani, flame tree, jasmine and bougainvillea which we obtained from the university nursery. However we could not succeed with a vegetable garden as much of the top soil had been removed. There are poisonous snakes locally so one had to be mindful when out gardening, or even just walking across the grass. Once our house boy killed a poisonous snake he found in our car port. Sadly a farmer admitted to hospital did not survive a snake bite as the poison had already spread before arrival.

At the Seventh Day Adventist hospital I was assigned a large open medical ward. This was not so different from my very early experience as a student nurse at Toronto General Hospital. The country had just conquered a cholera pandemic, but people were still being admitted to the hospital with cholera. It was a steep learning curve for me but I quickly learned the standard treatment for cholera. As long as we were able to obtain an intravenous access patients survived. The hospital was able to keep an adequate supply of intravenous fluids and drugs so we rarely lost a patient. The hospital operated with student nurses, a few registered nurses and midwives, and a few foreign doctors. The lack of qualified staff was stressful for me as our patients could be critically ill. However, the school of nursing was good and supported the students who worked hard. I worked closely with the two excellent nursing tutors.

During our first few years in Nigeria my family and I made several road trips. We travelled to Onitsha to attend the funeral of the grandmother of a friend. This trip was especially memorable as I saw remnants of the war. Driving was challenging as the road was badly cratered. Destroyed weaponry could be seen in the fields. The bridge over the River had yet to be repaired and we had to cross a temporary construction joining the bridge to the shore. My heart was in my mouth as my husband negotiated a narrow space congested with heavily laden lorries while the boys sang the River Niger song. Shortly after crossing the river we arrived at the city of Onitsha, a large commercial centre well-known for its covered central marketplace. My friend's grandmother had been a successful business woman operating in the East and Central Regions of Nigeria. Her funeral was very grand in keeping with her status. It was interesting to me to observe Igbo customs.

Many times we traveled to towns or villages in the region attending weddings but more often funerals, as many of our friends' parents had reached that time in their lives. If it was a family event our sons would accompany us otherwise they stayed home. Sometimes we had accommodation and could sleep before returning home, but other times we partied all night. The parties were held outside where tables and chairs were set up on the street. There was music and dancing which I enjoyed, joining with other guests to move with the rhythm. One thing I did not enjoy was having to stay up all night as I ran out of energy. If that happened, I would sneak off to the car for a nap. This did not impress my husband.

Another memorable road trip was to Kano in the North. At the start of our journey we heard on the radio the shocking news that there had been a military coup and General Obasanjo was now Head of State. However, this event did not affect our journey. When we stopped in Bida, well known for its glass and brass works, a student approached us at the gas station and offered to be our tour guide. We accepted his offer and he took us to visit a glass furnace where beads of varying shapes and colours were created from glass waste, and then we went on to the brass works. Our trip continued uneventfully passing by Kaduna and northward to Kano. In Kano we visited the marketplace moving from vendor to vendor (all male as the city is strongly Muslim) taking in the variety and beauty of local crafts such as leather products and traditional cotton blankets. We walked by the palace of the Emir of Kano, and our sons enjoyed a swim in the diving pool. We returned to Ife with a collection souvenir crafts.

My hospital employment required that I register with the Nursing and Midwifery Council of Nigeria. To accomplish this my professional colleague, Moji, and I went to Lagos bringing all my relevant documents. My husband provided a car and a driver. We were able to access the Council and achieve my goal of registration. On our return journey I wanted to stop in Ikorodu to greet my mother and father-in-law. When we arrived at the house, we were told to enter the house quickly. We were unaware that the town's Magbo festival was in progress, women and outsiders are forbidden to be seen on the streets during this time. This was actually a serious matter and we could have come to harm. However I was able to enjoy a pleasant visit with my in-laws. When it was time to leave, the driver readied the car and Moji and I quickly entered, crouching low in the back and covering ourselves with a cloth. When we had driven out of the town we sat up and laughed with relief.

Professionally, I traveled by road with two senior colleagues to attend a nursing conference in Bauchi. Near the start of the trip the van got stuck in mud on a road that was still under construction. With experience of pushing cars stuck in snow I joined in to 'heave ho'. After rocking the van back and forth many times we succeeded in releasing the van from the mud. Later in the journey we were directed to take this very bad road full of potholes. It was getting late so we stopped in a town where there was an old colonial guest house. Only one room with a queen size bed was available. The three of us managed to squeeze onto the bed together. I slept soundly! So the trip was quite the adventure, I can't remember the conference but our destination was Bauchi.

It was my first naming ceremony. Friends who lived at the bottom of the street recently had a baby girl, and for a girl the naming ceremony was to be held eight days after her birth. The ceremony took place at 7am.

I went alone. It was still dawn when I arose and dressed in traditional Yoruba attire of *buba* and *iro*. The cloth was a pretty pale pink cotton covered with colourful embroidery. Naming ceremonies follow a specific local ritual with traditional blessings spoken to the family and child. Items/foodstuff such as honey, kola nut, and a book were laid out on the table. One by one the elder conducting the ceremony described each item's significance to all present, a blessing was said and then the child tasted or touched each item one at a time. At the end of the ceremony the newborn, our friends' child, now had some new names and was now part of the community. We in the community now had a responsibility for this new member. After this joyous occasion I returned home only to discover that I had worn my clothing inside out. I laughed.

In 1976 the University of Ife with its vision of comprehensive health care, created the University of Ife Teaching Hospitals Complex (Obafemi Awolowo University Teaching Hospitals). Registered nurses and midwives were hired. Medical specialists, mainly Nigerians arrived at the university and set about providing specialist care. This improvement in health/medical care was a boon to the people of Ife. We the staff benefited with a salary increase as it was now a federal institution. Thus the creation of the teaching hospital complex benefitted staff and the surrounding community and was for the most part greeted with enthusiasm. I was happy to be a part of these changes.

Being in a leadership position in the hospital I needed to extend my qualifications. I applied and was accepted to study midwifery at the University College Hospital, Ibadan starting September 1977. My husband was supportive as we were both committed to our work. During my stay in Ibadan my husband cared for our two sons with the help of a 'house boy', and my friend who was visiting for a year. Earlier, we had moved to campus very close to the primary school so the boys were able to walk to and from school on their own. They enjoyed campus life, having the freedom to explore and play with their friends after lunch. The rule was that they had to be home before dusk. So despite missing them I felt comfortable that they were being looked after in my absence. I tried to come home as often as possible, taking public transit from Ibadan to Ife and negotiating getting from the university entrance to our house. For scheduled holidays I arranged with my husband so that he or a driver would bring me to Ife. As for my husband, he took advantage of my absence to have a liaison with an expatriate single woman. To my surprise mutual friends invited me over to congratulate me on accepting a second wife. My husband did not intend to marry this woman, so that relationship ended with my return.

Since my nursing school days I had wanted to become a midwife so I was very happy. At the School of Midwifery I was older than the other students, and one of only two women who were not Yoruba. I befriended Elizabeth who was from the East. She was fluent in Yoruba and I became indebted her for helping me with the Yoruba language. My vocabulary improved allowing me limited communication with the women I helped to care for. Elizabeth and I managed to arrange to work together at a local government maternity for one of our clinical placements. I enjoyed her company and our mutual support.

It was often expressed that the people believed that you went to a hospital to die and thus they often did not seek care until they were critically ill thus confirming the belief. However when the Oyo State government introduced free health care for a short period, the antenatal clinic became inundated with women wanting to receive maternity care through the hospital. Once free hospital care was discontinued women stayed away. This clearly indicated to me that the problem of deferring/avoiding hospital care until the condition was life threatening was more economic than cultural.

One day my colleagues came to inform me that a driver had come for me from the University of Ife. What a shock. A dear friend was dead, obstetrical hemorrhage. She was just 39 years old with three children. She was so full of life. I accompanied the driver back to Ife. He had the unpleasant task of relaying the bad news and dealing with a distraught passenger. I had only been in the country three years but my family had forged a friendship with Gbonju and her family. I was looking forward to many years of enjoying their friendship. Gbonju was a well-loved member of the University of Ife community. People had rushed to donate blood, anything to save her life. We were young and so full of energy and hope for the future. I very much felt both a part and apart of this community. Many people had known the family for many more years than myself, and conversation flowed in both English and Yoruba. However it was devastating for all of us to lose this friend/mother in the prime of her life. Friends and kin gathered at their home providing support for her husband and children. There was mutual support as we all processed this event and coped with our bereavement together. It was a very powerful process that we were moving through. If someone new arrived and was out of sync, the group would quickly let them know that we had moved beyond that stage. People shared memories, talking day and night. Women shopped and cooked for the group. This continued until the funeral. It was an overwhelmingly emotional experience for me. The funeral service and burial provided some closure but of course that is not the ending, but the beginning of redefining our lives and relationships. The myth of invincible youth was dashed in the realization that hope and youth could not guarantee a future

I returned to Ibadan immersing myself in my studies to ease the weight of sadness. After fourteen months of intense classroom teaching and clinical practice we wrote our exams for the Nursing and Midwifery Council of Nigeria. I was thankful for the support from the hospital Sisters, midwives and school Tutors. It was a very fulfilling experience. I was a proud graduate of the UCH School of Midwifery. Our graduating class was photographed and interviewed for Oyo State television. For some time after the graduation, whenever the TV was covering a health story, there I was on the screen among my graduating class. After completing the midwifery program I returned to the University of Ife Teaching Hospital Complex where I was assigned to the State hospital campus, to take charge of the Female Ward. Later I was to put my midwifery knowledge to practice as senior ward sister of the Labour Ward, eventually becoming a matron.

Our elder son, Lanre, was now in Primary 5 and decisions about secondary school needed to be made. My husband was a product of Government College, Ibadan and strongly wanted our sons to attend boarding school. At that time the secondary schools at Ife were not top quality. Despite my initial worries about sending a 10 year old to boarding school, we started to make preparations. Our son started working hard, studying with two friends to prepare for the entrance exams. He applied to three or four schools, and we drove him to the interviews. He was accepted at Federal Government College Ilorin. Thus began a long relationship with the school as Lanre's two cousins and younger brother later succeeded in gaining admission. The school was a pleasant two and a half hour journey from our home in Ife using the secondary highways. Visits were limited to designated visiting days and holidays. I often traveled there alone, my husband leaving that responsibility to me. I used the opportunities to bring some canned proteins and take the boys out to eat. The boys thrived but I missed having them at home. As a mother I felt disconnected, there was a vacuum.

This feeling of disconnection was aggravated by my husband spending less and less time at home. My husband was an engineer and travelled often as he sat on company boards in Lagos, and later in Benue state. I was proud of the work he was doing. However when home, more and more he would be out all evening usually playing squash and socializing. I found it difficult with working fulltime to both prepare supper and to accompany him to the squash courts to watch for the entire evening. It was not sustainable, we were on two separate schedules. This behavior was accentuated when both of our sons were at boarding school. I dealt with the isolation by spending more time at the staff club. Swimming was no longer an option due to the inability to obtain chemicals for the pool, so I took up tennis. I had played before but not for many years. A few women had started to play tennis making the tennis courts a much friendlier and welcoming place. The tennis club held tournaments and I enjoyed traveling with the club to compete at the Ibadan Recreation Club. They had clay courts, a surface on which I had first learned to play tennis. It was fun for me playing a couple of matches. So the Staff Club was a place for me to socialize, and to participate in games such as darts and scrabble. It was a great place to de-stress after work and cope with a husband who was distancing himself.

Another way I filled the void was to become more involved in my professional life. Two of my colleagues invited me to join them in delivering an educational program for teenagers on reproductive health. We would go to different schools in the area to educate the students who volunteered to attend for a few sessions. Also, for a couple of academic sessions I taught reproductive health to community health students. Later I became an examiner for the Nursing and Midwifery Council of Nigeria. This involved conducting the written and oral nursing or midwifery examinations as a member of the team for the Council. Most of the time I examined locally but also had the opportunity to travel to Benin City, Abeokuta and Lagos. I enjoyed meeting other professional colleagues and visiting other hospitals.

Safety on the highways had become a major topic for discussion, especially the dangers of driving after dark. Thieves waylaid travelers usually at night and there was the danger of lorries driving without lights. University staff had been losing their life on the roads. In response to this, Prof. Wole Soyinka, a prominent academician and Nobel Prize winning author, made an effort to address highway safety on the Ife-Ibadan highway. There was initial enthusiasm for his plans but without political will it was not sustainable. As for thieves, both my husband and I experienced their audacity. The first time was when I had taken my son to the hospital for diagnostic tests. When we finished and were ready to go home my car was no longer where I parked it. The security officer had allowed the thieves to drive away with my car. This was more than a temporary inconvenience as I depended on my car to get to work. I reported the theft to the police but said they could do nothing. For I short while I relied on a colleague to pick me up on her way to the hospital. On another occasion thieves managed to enter campus and confronted my husband at the Staff Club parking lot. There they smashed his glasses and drove off with his car. The thieves later used the car to engage in robberies in town. The police had a shootout with the robbers and recovered the car. Not having a car on campus made life very difficult as distances were far and there was no public transit .This was the era before cell phones and land lines were rare, so communication was in person. After some months of having to manage work and home without a car, thankfully, my husband was able to buy another car for me. Alone at home one evening, a couple came to the door informing me that the car carrying our two sons had broken down and was parked on the Ife -Ibadan road. I drove out alone and was able to rescue them without any incident.

My father-in-law came from Ikorodu to visit. It was an honour for me. He stayed with us for a week. When he arrived, I had a fleeting feeling that he was coming to say goodbye. Our older son was at boarding school but our younger son was at home and so was able to spend some time with his grandfather. My husband made himself scarce so the responsibility of caring and entertaining my father-in-law fell to me. I was annoyed with my husbands' behavior but was determined to ensure his father had a very pleasant visit. I took him to the staff club to meet many friends and I entertained a few close friends at home. Before he left a close family friend expressed the same feeling that I had, that "Baba" had come to say good-bye. Later that year my father-in-law died.

As my father-in-law had been a bureaucrat in the Western State, and later Lagos state governments, he was well respected in the community. He had had several wives, my husband's mother being the senior wife, many children and a large extended family. Thus his funeral was to be a grand occasion. A family meeting was held at his home to determine each member's contribution and responsibilities, to choose the cloth family members would wear, and to set the date. When the date came, the celebrations started with the wake on Friday evening. Saturday was the funeral service at the Methodist Church followed by a parade to the burial grounds. We the mourners walked through the town following a marching band and the hearse to the cemetery. Prayers were said and hymns were sung as my father-in-law was lowered into the grave. We returned to the house where the family was to entertain their guests with tables and chairs set up on the street. As a wife of the family I was expected to help with the buying of food stuff, overseeing the cooking, and entertaining the friends we would invite. This was a real challenge for me. While the women of the family knew exactly what to do and moved quickly to secure food for themselves and their friends, I on the other hand was unprepared and my lack of fluency was an impediment. So I was left struggling to obtain sufficient food and seating space to entertain our friends. At one point, I felt so frustrated and inadequate, I was in tears. After my little 'melt-down' I relaxed and settled in to enjoy the occasion as I had managed to garner adequate refreshments for our guests. Four steers had been slaughtered for the occasion and as was the custom, meat was apportioned out and delivered to the town dignitaries. The party continued well into the night. The celebrations came to a conclusion with the thanksgiving service at the Methodist Church on the Sunday, following which we returned to Ife.

When my mother-in-law died a few years later I was more prepared and did not experience the same feeling of being an outsider. However my lack of fluency in the Yoruba language was still an issue for me. Our boys had not been able to attend Baba's funeral, but this time we made sure they were released from school and were able to attend this important family event.

In my professional career I became very involved with the local chapter of the National Association of Nigeria Nurses and Midwives, being elected to an executive position. I occasionally traveled to Ibadan for meetings or educational workshops. As a union member, I joined with other unions including the Academic Staff Union to march against an injustice by the military government. Once, in response to the Union who had dared to challenge the government, the military came with their weaponry to block the entrance to the university with a tank. This was a tense period on campus as the government clamped down on their opponents and sent their agents onto the campus to search out and arrest the Union leaders. The fear was very real as the military had the power to incarcerate civilian opponents and kill military opponents. However, the tension gradually subsided as the government resorted to other means to muzzle the power of the academic staff union. Subsequent strikes and closures of the university occurred in tandem. The closures seriously affected the school year so that it no longer ran from September to May. They disrupted student learning, delayed graduation, and had an impact on students pursuing postgraduate education. This was the state of things when I left Nigeria.

It was so nice when my mother and her husband came to visit. We brought them to Ife for the week. Our sons were home for the holidays and thus were able to spend the time with their Grandmother. They enjoyed their stay on campus as we entertained them, touring the Oni of Ife's palace and other historical sites. My sister-in-law and her husband held a party for my mother at their home in Lagos inviting some other family members. It was a special occasion for my mother. Their departure from Nigeria was particularly memorable for them. A military coup had just taken place and as we drove to the airport in Lagos we met tanks on the highway as the coup leaders asserted their control of the government. General Buhari was declared Head of State and the 'War on Indiscipline' was launched.

Apart from military coups, there were two elections that I experienced. It was quieter than usual when I drove to work the morning following the first election. Work started normally but then we could hear gunshots outside the compound. Support staff started to disappear so it appeared we had to shut down hospital operations to the bare minimum so that staff living on the compound could handle the situation. This took some time and effort. When I was ready to leave with one of my staff who had stayed to help. I was anxious and fearful but believed I would come to no harm. As we drove into town I had to negotiate around some barriers. People were on their balconies keeping watch. I dropped off my colleague and continued through a back route to campus, giving a local resident a lift to his mechanic. After dropping him off I was confronted by three young men. The road was so badly potholed I could only drive very slowly, so they stopped me and demanded money. One man even jumped into the car with a machete. I was able to negotiate his exit on agreeing to give him money, which I did. I drove on as fast as I could until I came up to a road block. I saw a hospital worker on a balcony and asked her what to say to be allowed to pass through the barrier. So I approached and shouted out 'Awo' and was allowed to pass which I did quickly before they changed their minds. I drove straight to the Staff Club to let my husband and friends know that I was safe. They were happy to see me. They were also checking to make sure other staff were safely back on campus. Fortunately, in Ife, the 1988 election was not accompanied by such violence.

My father and his wife had visited us a few years earlier. Disappointingly they only had a weekend in Nigeria on a stop-over so I arranged an hotel room for them in Lagos. We had a brief but pleasant time together. They were able to see a little of Lagos and meet some of my husband's family.

After living in Nigeria for fourteen years, I travelled to Canada for our brother's wedding, and to celebrate my father's 70th birthday. By this time my husband had become more estranged. So when I left Nigeria to attend those family events it became apparent to me that the future for myself and our sons would not be in Nigeria. I initially requested a leave of absence from the hospital hoping for reconciliation but later retired as it was apparent that my husband's eyes were elsewhere and my efforts were useless. However my husband was able to help as I worked towards transferring our elder son from the University of Ife to the University of Toronto. With some ground work his younger brother was offered admission to his university of choice. The three of us, not without a sense of loss, looked forward to a new life in Canada.

I had experienced a very full life in Nigeria being fully engaged in my professional life, raising our sons, socializing with many friends, and over time feeling more a part of my husbands' family and Yoruba culture. I enjoyed the opportunity to travel to many different corners of Nigeria. Despite living in Canada I am still a wife of my husband's family and continue to have a relationship with the family. In 1999 I traveled to Nigeria to attend my nephew-in-law's wedding and stayed one month with my sister-in-law. When I walked into my sister-in-law's house I felt like I was home.

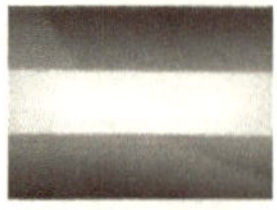

Insider or Outsider
Negotiating Life in Nigeria

Eliane Mbodwam

My husband, Dick, and I met and were married in Addis Ababa, Ethiopia in 1969. We moved to Nigeria in 1977 with the first two of our four children and when I was pregnant with our third child. But let me first tell you a little of my background.

I was born towards the end of WW2 in Sarreguemines, a small town in North Eastern France right on the border between France and Germany. When I was born in January 1944, it was under German occupation. Three months earlier the Allied Forces had bombed the town and one bomb fell on the house where my parents lived. My mother, who was six months pregnant with me, was buried under rubble in the cellar. By the Providence of God we both survived. My only sibling, Suzanne, was born six years later.

Before entering Kindergarten at age 4, I spoke mostly our local dialect which has much in common with the language spoken on the other side of the border, in Saarland. Although I hardly speak it now I still remember and understand it.

I had a carefree and happy childhood and enjoyed going on hiking trips and holidays with my parents and my younger sister. We also had a garden not far from our apartment where we were growing vegetables: Irish potatoes, carrots, cabbage, tomatoes, and green beans. My sister and I spent many happy hours there playing and helping our parents to remove weeds in the garden and harvest the fruit and vegetables. There were two large pear trees, several plum trees and cherry trees and a peach tree as well as strawberries, blackberries, raspberries, red and black currants. When they were in season we provided our neighbours with peaches, pears and red currants and my mother made delicious jelly from the red currants and raspberries.

On the way to our garden we always passed what was left of two WW2 bunkers where my parents and many other people had taken shelter from the bombs during the war. My parents told me that when I was just a few months old we had stayed in the bunker for as long as three weeks. Whenever it appeared safe to go out my father would take his bike and go to a nearby village to buy some milk and other provisions. Meanwhile, my baby cousin and I slept comfortably in the bomb shelter in a cozy laundry basket, unaware of what must have been a very difficult time for many people.

I was baptized and confirmed in the Lutheran Church of Alsace-Lorraine. When I was older I enjoyed attending the weekly Mixed Youth gatherings. Each year our Parish organized a camp for young people over the age of 14. The first one I attended was in Belgium. It was there I first discovered the sea. I remember how excited I was. The following year we went to Holland, then to Italy. The last camp I attended was in Spain about 80km south of Barcelona. We really enjoyed the warm weather and water of the Mediterranean Sea. Against the advice of our pastor's wife, a small group of us joined our bus driver at the local bull fight arena. It was an interesting experience although I can't say I really enjoyed it.

I attended kindergarten, primary and secondary school in my home town. Sarreguemines had been badly damaged during the war and many buildings had been destroyed including schools. Temporary wooden buildings were constructed to house kindergarten and primary schools. They were not so well insulated and in winter we had to have a wood and coal burning stove in the classroom to keep us warm and to heat the milk the government provided for us. I remember one particularly cold winter when the ink froze in the small ink wells in our desks. My primary school years were easy and I was always at the top of my class.

After completing secondary school I proceeded to Strasbourg to attend a two-year course leading to a Trilingual Secretary Diploma (French, German, and English). During my second year of studying in

Strasbourg I heard about a Lutheran radio station in Addis Ababa, Ethiopia from a lady pastor whose son was setting up a French language department there. The station's leadership was looking for a bilingual secretary who was also interested in broadcasting Christian and educational programs for French speaking audiences in Africa. I was invited for an interview, but my parents were not in favour of letting me go to Africa when I was only about 20 years old. However two years later as the position remained vacant I was asked to reconsider. My parents seemed less opposed to the idea of my going to Africa and by July 1966 all was set for me to travel to Addis Ababa for an initial three year contract. My parents accompanied me to Frankfurt airport where I boarded an Ethiopian Airlines plane to Addis Ababa via Athens and Cairo. Little did I know that the three years would turn into over ten years and that I would meet my life partner there and spend the rest of my life in Africa.

I started work at the very powerful and busy Lutheran radio station in Addis Ababa, called Radio Voice of the Gospel (RVOG). A number of "feeder studios" located in Eastern, Southern and Western Africa as well as in Madagascar, Lebanon, India, Pakistan and even China produced programs in their languages, recorded them on tape and shipped them to the transmitter station in Addis Ababa to be broadcast back to audiences in their countries on its two powerful one hundred kilowatt shortwave transmitters located 20 miles out of Addis Ababa. All these tapes arrived at the "Traffic Office" whose staff was responsible for putting the right programs on at the right times for the right target audiences. A master news bulletin was prepared in English by the chief news editor and then translated and read live by the language editors. I also got a chance to prepare and present the news in French. In 1968 a daily news bulletin in the Hausa language was added. The civil war was going on in Nigeria at the time and people there relied heavily on RVOG for reliable and credible information. This brought about the arrival of a young man from Jos, Nigeria named Dick Mbodwam. And my life changed.

Dick and I soon became close friends and before long Dick expressed the desire to marry me. However, he was already engaged to a Danish missionary back in Nigeria. At last he decided to inform his fiancée that he had met a French girl who stole his heart and he broke the engagement. We were now free to marry and our wedding was set for April 1969 in Addis Ababa.

When I told my family about my marriage plans they were not thrilled that I was marrying an African man, but they didn't veto it. However I regret that my parents and sister decided not to come to Addis Ababa to witness our marriage. One reason they gave was the language barrier as none spoke or understood English. No one from Dick's family was present either. We got married at the International Lutheran Church. The ceremony was conducted in both English and French. It was the first, but not the last interracial marriage at RVOG.

For eight years we lived on the RVOG compound in a bungalow located at the top of the hill and we enjoyed quite a beautiful view over the city. I continued working full time and enjoyed preparing and recording programs for French speaking audiences in West Africa, though I had never been there. During this time Anne and Sam, the first two of our four children, were born. It was not difficult to continue working because we had a househelper/cook and a nurse to take care of the children during the day. Any time my attention was needed at home the househelper/ nurse would call me on the phone and I could get home quickly.

My first visit to Nigeria was for a three-month furlough at the end of the Nigerian civil war with our two-year old daughter Anne. We arrived in Lagos and I was struck by how very different Lagos was from Addis Ababa. So many more people and cars on the streets! And so much warmer than Addis Ababa! We only stayed two days and then took a domestic flight to Jos. I enjoyed the slower pace of life there and the beautiful Plateau landscape with lots of large rock formations. Some were quite spectacular. It was late November when we arrived and I experienced Harmattan season for the first time. Harmattan is the name of the dry cool wind blowing from the North and carrying fine dust from the Sahara desert. You could wipe dust from furniture several times a day!

After about two weeks in Jos where we stayed on the compound of Muryar Bishara (Voice of the Gospel in Hausa) recording studio we were ready to make the long road journey to Numan, Dick's home town, and where at last I would meet his family. I had already met Dick's father, Catechist Obida Mbodwam, in Ethiopia when he had the opportunity to include a visit to his son in Addis Ababa on his way home from visiting Denmark. We were not yet married when he came and I recall how eager I was to make a good impression on him. He had asked me to help him buy a shirt for himself and I had been a bit unsure of myself as at first I thought he wanted shorts and not a shirt and I didn't know where to go to buy shorts. Now we were about to meet Dick's mother and his nine siblings for the first time.

We had bought a second hand car in Jos and drove the 450 kilometers to Numan, located where the Rivers Benue (a tributary of the Niger) and Gongola merge. The road from Jos to Bauchi (about 120kms) was in poor condition and quite narrow. Half way between Jos and Bauchi we had to climb Pan Shanu, a pass between two high hills. At the top we stopped and looked down and we saw a new road being constructed. (Three years later we drove through what was a hill that had been blasted to make a way for a beautiful and smooth three lane road.) The last 50 km before Numan were also rough with many pot holes and once when we were going uphill we had to stop and let the engine cool. I was a bit nervous since we appeared to be in a very isolated area and I was imagining that wild animals or bandits might appear any time. However, before long we approached Numan and Dick pointed out to me the steeple of his church. At this time, in 1971, there was no bridge to cross the River Benue at Numan and we became concerned that it was getting late and we would not make it on time for the crossing of the last ferry of the day. We arrived there around 6 pm just as it started getting dark. Dick's father had crossed over in a canoe earlier and was looking out for us. We had a joyful reunion with him there at the crowded edge of the river. A number of cars and lorries were also waiting to cross before dark. A minor accident had caused some delay but at last we drove on to the ferry and headed towards Numan. I was quite nervous as the ferry did not appear very strong and I had heard stories of hippos and crocodiles in the river. However after about 15 minutes we had crossed safely.

After a short drive we entered the mission compound where we were welcomed by Dick's mother, siblings and other relations. The younger ones all spoke English but the older folks spoke only Bachama (the tribal language) and Hausa. I didn't understand either unfortunately, but people were very gracious and understanding.

We stayed in a small house on the Mission compound. It was nicknamed the "Doll House". I felt comfortable there because several Danish missionaries and their families lived on the compound and we were often invited for dinner or afternoon coffee and cake.

It was early December and the cotton harvest was in full swing as well as the millet harvest. People were busy making preparations for

Christmas; sewing new clothes for the whole family and buying new shoes, making new fences from grass mats, slaughtering cows, sheep, goats and chicken. Christmas is the time of the year when people travel to their hometowns from near and far to be with their relations. So it was a good time for us to meet many of Dick's extended family and friends.

In March of 1977 I was expecting our third child when the Ethiopian Military Government took over RVOG and all expatriates working there left to return to their home countries. We prepared to leave for Nigeria. The management of the station arranged for professional packers to pack all our belongings under the vigilant eye of 2 or 3 soldiers. Thankfully it all happened in a rather relaxed manner. Still, I felt a bit uneasy about it all.

We arrived Jos on April 9th, 1977 and settled into Jos, the picturesque city we had visited briefly during our first trip to Nigeria. We moved on the Muyrar Bishara compound where we had stayed during our first visit. Dick was appointed the new director, I gave birth to our second daughter, Grace, in July, we put the two older children in school and we settled in to our new Nigerian environment. I was staying at home taking care of baby Grace. This was quite a change after having been working full time for over 10 years and having a househelper/cook and a nurse to help with the children. Otherwise, my environment was quite similar to that of Addis Ababa with expatriate missionaries on the compound.

We did hire a cook whose expatriate employer was on furlough. He spoke only Pidgin English and I remember wondering what he meant when he asked me if he should "kill the potatoes" that were cooking on the gas stove. When I finally understood that he was asking if he should turn the potatoes off, l laughed so hard that my ribs started hurting. Up till now I get the giggles when I remember. While Dick was in England on an 8-week management course, one of his sisters came to stay with me. She was a nurse and came to Jos to attend a midwifery course. A lady whose husband was employed at Muryar Bishara studio helped me in the home.

Within two years we moved four times, but then we stayed in the same house on the Muryar Bishara compound for the next 40 years!

In September 1980 on our way to France, our whole family visited some good friends in Denmark. We had been together with them briefly in Addis Ababa and for a longer period in Jos. From there we moved to Lyon in France where Dick attended a three-month international course in mass media communication. We stayed in a flat on the 8th floor of an apartment building. Thank goodness there was a lift in the building. During this time, Anne and Sam attended a French school and Grace went to a nearby Kindergarten. Only the youngest, Emmanuel who turned one while we were there, was at home. Dick seemed to enjoy his course in France. Most classes were conducted in English.

Funny enough, I found it quite scary to drive in France though I had been driving confidently in Ethiopia and Jos. I was afraid I would break some traffic rules and be pulled over by the police. So I bought a booklet to review traffic rules but I was still quite nervous and didn't venture very far, mostly just for grocery shopping. My parents came all the way from Sarreguemines by train to visit us for a week. And on the weekend of November 1st my sister and her family drove down from Germany in their Toyota camper van. It was All Saints Day so I went with our children to the nearby graveyard to see all the beautiful flowers people put on the graves of their deceased relatives. It is quite a sight!

At my suggestion we spent Christmas in Lyon before returning to Nigeria thinking we would all enjoy a French Christmas. However, it turned out to be a bit of a disappointment as we celebrated it all by ourselves. I believe Dick, and the older children too, missed all the church activities and exuberance that accompanies Christmas in Nigeria. Unfortunately a Christmas in France was only meaningful to me!

Back in Jos in January 1981 Anne and Sammy continued schooling at Hillcrest, a mission school with an American curriculum. It was a challenge to pay their fees despite the reduction we enjoyed due to our affiliation with the Lutheran Church of Christ in Nigeria which is one of the missions associated with Hillcrest school. Grace attended Kindergarten at a local Nigerian school.

The 80s were a difficult period with the Structural Adjustment Program which the Nigerian Government had recently adopted. Prices of commodities went up considerably and I remember getting worried that our family might experience famine. Relief came when I resumed working. After a short spell working as a secretary at a private school, I started working part time at the Muryar Bishara studio. Then I had the opportunity to teach at Hillcrest School. That was a great blessing as I was being paid in US dollars and we enjoyed a substantial rebate on our children's school fees. I felt honored to be entrusted with that job since I had no previous teaching experience. The faculty members and administration were very kind and patient and helped me in many ways. I look back with pride and gratitude for those nearly 10 years.

Each of our four children left Nigeria after finishing secondary school and embarked on studies in universities in the USA. The departure from home of Emmanuel, our last born, left a huge void in my life. It took me quite some time to get used to the empty nest. It was a relief when my husband's niece, Mori, who had been a close buddy of our daughter Grace, came to stay with us. She is still with us today, although her presence in the house has required some adjustments on my part. I am still learning to practice patience and to appreciate having her with us, as she is doing most of the cooking which I do not enjoy doing, to say the least.

There had been minor ethnic and religious conflicts in Jos earlier, but starting on September 11th, 2001 we experienced a major crisis. We had heard all kinds of rumors of pending attacks by Hausa Muslims prior to that day but we didn't pay too much attention to them until Muslims started attacking Christians and Christians began retaliating. The fighting went on for more than a week and the loss of life and destruction of properties on both sides were considerable. We were particularly vulnerable because the area in which our Muryar Bishara compound was located had gradually become largely inhabited by Hausa Muslims. One day young men armed with clubs and machetes who were among those attacking Christians nearby tried to come into our compound but to our relief they didn't succeed. Many Christians sought refuge on our compound.

On the third day it appeared calm had been restored in our city and I ventured out with the car to the house of some friends on the other side of town to use their email to communicate with our children. Along the way I was shocked by the sight of carcasses of cars that had been set on fire and buildings that had been destroyed by fire. The following day fighting broke out again and we stayed home under a 24 hour curfew lasting several days.

Although the Muslims had attacked Christians and many Christians had retaliated, when it was over we heard stories of many instances of Christians giving refuge to Muslims and Muslims rescuing Christians from attacks. Sadly however, after the crisis the city of Jos became a divided city with Christians and Muslims moving to separate parts of Jos. Unfortunately for us before long many more Muslims bought land and built houses on all sides of our compound and we ended up living in an isolated Christian compound. We felt very vulnerable and I learned to pray earnestly for God's protection and for peace of mind and heart.

Another serious crises took place in November 2008. Because of our location within the Muslim part of Jos, some soldiers came to escort us to a predominately Christian area of the city. Since our son Emmanuel, who was teaching at Hillcrest and living on the Hillcrest compound with his family, were in France at the time, I was able to stay in their apartment along with my English friend who had been visiting me from Yola. While we were there a French man who was in charge of the safety of French nationals in Jos even brought us some French military rations. After three days we were told it was safe enough for us to return home. But because of the tension, my husband suggested I travel to Yola with my English friend. After a week in Yola, I decided to return to Jos to prepare for Christmas as it was already December 11. On my way back I got the good news that Kahindo, the wife of our son Emmanuel, had given birth safely to a baby girl, our 7th grandchild!

After the 2008 Jos crisis our children pleaded with us to relocate either to France or the US where we would be safer. After some soul searching and a lot of discussions involving my husband's relations, in 2010 we decided to leave Nigeria and move to Southern France since Emmanuel and his family had settled in Marseille and my sister also lived in the area. We agreed that I should go first and see how we could settle there. When an apartment became vacant in the house where Emmanuel and his family were living, we took that as a positive sign. We packed up most of our belongings (though we left some to be shipped later), I said goodbye to my friends. Ready for that new adventure, I left Nigeria by the end of April 2010. My husband joined me three months later. However, it didn't take us long to realize that we didn't really have the resources to live in France and it would be wiser to return to Nigeria. There we could use whatever resources we had to build a house in Jos. So a few months after Dick's arrival to France we again packed our bags and returned to Jos.

It took us a number of years to complete the house on land my husband had bought back in 2009. But with substantial help from our son, Samuel, on December 1st 2018 we finally moved into our own home. Needless to say we are very grateful to him. And it was really timely too as Dick had finally retired from The Lutheran Church of Christ in Nigeria, which he had served in various capacities for nearly 60 years, and we were expected to vacate the house on the Muryar Bishara compound.

We are now the proud grandparents of 12 precious grandchildren, 6 granddaughters and 6 grandsons! Unfortunately we do not get to see them very often. And when we see them it is sometimes difficult to relate to them meaningfully since most of them are growing up in a different world from ours. Hopefully some of them will come to visit Nigeria some day and see the place their mom or dad grew up. Wishful thinking? Perhaps!

Our family is really international with roots in four continents, Africa, Europe, Asia and America. We have in-laws from Vietnam, Congo (DRC), USA, Israel and El Salvador making us a seven-country family! I really wish we could have a grand family reunion someday; but it may only happen in heaven!

Having spent most of my life in Africa, 10 years in Ethiopia and over 40 years in Nigeria, I definitely feel more at home in Africa than in Europe or America. However I do sometimes wonder if I would stay in Nigeria should I survive my husband. Despite many years in Nigeria, I certainly have not become a *bona fide* Nigerian. I still think and react as a "baturiya" (white lady in Hausa) most of the time and I haven't acquired the Nigerian sense of humor. However, I am doing my best to not be rude or hurt the feelings of Nigerian friends and relations. Thank God most of them, and especially my husband, are very gracious and forgiving of my lapses, especially my failure to understand and speak Hausa properly and my notorious inability to remember people. I am most grateful to my husband for encouraging me to travel back to France occasionally to see members of my family and to the US to see our children and grandchildren and also for not expecting me to behave like a typical Nigerian wife.

The people who tried to caution me against marrying an African would often say that a person who grew up in Africa would have a very different perspective on marriage and life in general and that would constitute a big challenge. But we were young and in love and we brushed aside such concerns. I realise there is some truth in this. However he, and even his parents, had been exposed to western civilization through close contact with missionaries from Denmark. I believe this fact as well as our shared faith in God has been a very positive factor that contributed to the longevity of our marriage of 52 years!

And I do believe we made the right choice to stay in Nigeria instead of moving to Europe or the US, despite the many challenges and the present insecurity in the country. After all, there is no place in this world that is100% safe to live. I hope I will continue to integrate and absorb some of the good and positive values of the Nigerian culture such as emphasis on relationships and that I will learn to exercise patience and overlook minor offences. I am grateful that our children have a broader world view because of their interaction with different cultures while they were growing up. I can also say with confidence that my life has been enriched by experiencing the culture of Ethiopia and by over forty years of deep involvement in Nigeria as a Nigerwife.

Who are the Nigerwives?

Informally Nigerwives refers to any woman of non-Nigerian origin who is married to a Nigerian. Nigerwives also refers to a national association of foreign women married to Nigerians. The aims of the association are, among others, to facilitate the smooth integration of foreign wives of Nigerians into the Nigerian society and also to establish or assist in social projects of benefit to the Nigerian community. There are now about 300 members from 69 countries in 13 branches nationwide as well as in the UK and USA

Since 1995, Nigerwives-Nigeria, established the **Nigerwives Braille Book Production Centre (NWBBPC)**, a National Project, which has been providing Braille books for visually impaired students countrywide. It also provides computer training for blind graduates and has recently produced Braille Ballot Papers for Nigerian Elections

The Association has been of tremendous help to members in assisting them with getting jobs and being there in times of need. Regular monthly meetings keep members in touch with each other. Nigerian recipes, basic Nigerian culture and fashion such as the "head tie" are learned from friendly Nigerian ladies. We can now boast of being excellent cooks of Nigerian foods and divas of Nigerian fashion.

Drawn from the Nigerwives Website
https://nigerwives.wixsite.com › nigeria

In Memoriam

We acknowledge the unwritten stories of our departed sisters from Bulgaria, India, Ireland, Poland, Russia, and Trinidad who lived in Jos, Nigeria for many long years.

Yolanda Ehiedu

Molly Jibrin

Tina Juryit

Margaret Kebang

Tatiana Machunga

Tatiana Mohammed

Carol Pwajok

Eliamma Ugoh

Velma Uku

About the Editors

Kanchana Ugbabe is from Chenna, South India. She met her Nigerian husband in Australia and moved to Nigeria in 1975. She retired as professor of English after long years of teaching and mentoring students at the University of Jos. Ugbabe is also a creative writer who has published short stories in journals including a collection called *Soulmates*. (Penguin, 2011)

Joanne Umolu is from the USA. She met her husband in Germany and moved to Nigeria in1965. She worked as a teacher for forty years in southern and northern Nigeria. She retired as a professor of Special Education from the University of Jos in 1999 and has since been involved in promoting literacy development and special education activities in Nigeria